"Mark Nepo will guide you to the very source of your own creative spirit and inspire you to inhabit, trust, and express its radiance. This beautiful book is a gift on the journey of awakening."

TARA BRACH
author of *Radical Acceptance*
and *True Refuge*

"Hundreds of thousands of readers, including me, have found new life in Mark Nepo's writing. We know that a great 'river of light' flows through this good man and out into artistic expression. In this heartfelt and beautiful book, Mark aims to help his readers find the river of light within themselves and learn how it wants to express itself. As Mark says, 'all forms of expression . . . are meant to awaken the love that is possible in the world.' Want to become a bearer of love and light in a world that too many find dark and loveless? This new offering by a spiritual virtuoso of our era will help you find the way."

PARKER J. PALMER
author of *On the Brink of Everything*,
Healing the Heart of Democracy,
and *Let Your Life Speak*

"I love all of Mark Nepo's books, but this one is especially beautiful, luminous, wise, and helpful—a river of light for the thirsty traveler. We need beacons of light to guide us through these times. Mark offers a river." ELIZABETH LESSER
cofounder of the Omega Institute
and author of *The Seeker's Guide*,
Broken Open, and *Marrow*

"Sacred seeing is an art, and creative expression is a sacrament. In *Drinking from the River of Light*, Mark Nepo invites us into a living encounter with the Holy, as the birthright of all humans in relationship with the wild beauty of creation. As a writer dedicated to naked authenticity, I cherish the wisdom and embrace the practices offered in this luminous book."

MIRABAI STARR
author of *Caravan of No Despair*
and *Wild Mercy*

"In *Drinking from the River of Light*, Mark Nepo's words land like dew on a thirsty leaf. He helps us see the artist within and takes the reader on a dance between oneself and Nepo's shared wisdom. I couldn't put it down and drank in every word of it."

ZAINAB SALBI
author of *Freedom Is an Inside Job*

"Mark Nepo's latest book is filled with achingly moving and poetic anecdotes, wise reminders, and terrific quotes you'll never find on quotes.com. The invitation is writ large among these pages to pay attention to the world (and your presence within it) in all its rough glory—to love the truth of what is, using whatever mode of expression enchants you—as your very gateway to the divine. This is a book of refined wisdom, insight, and great reminding. Crack the spine of this gem, drink fully from the river of light, and as Whitman advised, go forth to 'Sing the body electric!'"
ALBERT FLYNN DESILVER
author of *Writing as a Path of Awakening*

"As a poet, Mark Nepo commands language with a fierce truth that is difficult, if not impossible, to turn away from. His voice and person serve that light that shines so brightly in the darkest corners of the world."   RICHARD FRANKEL
Indiana University School of Medicine

"Mark Nepo is that rarest of literary birds: a Renaissance-style writer who dares to bring his whole hybrid self to the page—literary poet, unabashed mystic, homespun philosopher, cancer survivor, and impassioned seeker singing the glories of the world. This wonderful book is a deep dive into the universal art of self-expression, exploring how to give voice to our deepest, most original self in a world where we often feel unheard, and how to hear the voice of God in our own when we listen closely to what is inside us. Candid, rich, and consistently profound. I loved it."   MARK MATOUSEK
author of *Sex, Death, Enlightenment*
and *When You're Falling, Dive*

drinking
from the
river of
light

for Arianna,
with my love,

Also by Mark Nepo

NONFICTION
More Together Than Alone
Things That Join the Sea and the Sky
The One Life We're Given
The Endless Practice
Seven Thousand Ways to Listen
Finding Inner Courage
Unlearning Back to God
The Exquisite Risk
The Book of Awakening

FICTION
As Far As the Heart Can See

POETRY
The Way Under the Way
Inside the Miracle
Reduced to Joy
Surviving Has Made Me Crazy
Suite for the Living
Inhabiting Wonder
Acre of Light
Fire Without Witness
God, the Maker of the Bed, and the Painter

EDITOR
Deepening the American Dream

RECORDINGS
More Together Than Alone
Flames That Light the Heart (video course)
The One Life We're Given
Inside the Miracle (expanded, 2015)
Reduced to Joy
The Endless Practice
Seven Thousand Ways to Listen
Staying Awake
Holding Nothing Back
As Far As the Heart Can See
The Book of Awakening
Finding Inner Courage
Finding Our Way in the World
Inside the Miracle (1996)

drinking

from the

river of

light

the
life
of
expression

MARK NEPO

sounds true
BOULDER, COLORADO

Sounds True
Boulder, CO 80306

Published 2019

Book design by Beth Skelley

Printed in Canada

Library of Congress Cataloging-in-Publication Data

Names: Nepo, Mark, author.
Title: Drinking from the river of light : the life of expression / Mark Nepo.
Description: Boulder, CO : Sounds True, [2019] | Includes bibliographical
    references.
Identifiers: LCCN 2018050570 (print) | LCCN 2018059911 (ebook) |
    ISBN 9781683642312 (ebook) | ISBN 9781683642305 (pbk.)
Subjects: LCSH: Creation (Literary, artistic, etc.) | Self-actualization
    (Psychology)
Classification: LCC BF408 (ebook) | LCC BF408 .N675 2019 (print) |
    DDC 153.3/5—dc23
LC record available at https://lccn.loc.gov/2018050570

10 9 8 7 6 5 4 3 2 1

There are those who water
the seed of light that no one sees.
They are visionaries.

And those who hold others, feeling
the power of what they can become.
They are teachers.

And those who care enough
to love the truth of what-is
until Heaven is revealed
here on Earth.
They are sages.

Few are celebrities.
Few are rich.
The best
are often silent,
deflecting attention,
bowing to the gift.

This is for them
and their lineage
and the hope
that we can do this
for each other.

MN

You use a mirror to see your face,
you use art to see your soul.
GEORGE BERNARD SHAW

Contents

PART 1 BASIC HUMAN TRUTHS

Why Write

The Gift of Vision

The Art of Perception

The Chord in Our Heart

Understanding Practice

PART 4 BECOMING ONE WITH

The Magic of Liberty

The Timeless River

The River of Light

Both Leonardo da Vinci and Michelangelo left a trail of unfinished art greater than anyone else in modern history. Still, they are regarded as two of the most talented artists who ever lived. They are extraordinary examples of how the journey of expression is more important than the final product.

William Blake is another inspiring example. Toward the end of his life, Blake endeavored to illustrate Dante's *Divine Comedy*, the medieval epic poem that follows Dante's transformative journey through Hell and Purgatory into Paradise. Blake created 102 watercolors, planning to engrave them all, but he only had time to begin seven.

More than his immense effort to create art, Blake's innate devotion was to immerse himself deeply in the thickest currents of life. Though he couldn't finish engraving his illustrations, I imagine that, at some point, the life-force Blake was so devoted to began engraving him. What more can any of us ask for but to be created by the very thing we feel compelled to create? This is where the holy work of effort leads, regardless of its trail.

Recently, while in London, I stood before one of Blake's illustrations. It was a sketch of Dante on his knees, drinking from the River of Light, which descended from somewhere unseen like a waterfall. In this sketch, drawn three years before his death, Blake brought into being a portrait of himself. As I stood before it, over two hundred years later, I knew in my heart it was a portrait of me as well, and of every writer and teacher who ever lived.

For when we express, when we let out what is in, regardless of how, we are drinking from the River of Light. And that act, that devotion, allows us to glimpse the fabric of the Universe and the web of connection that holds life together. Glimpsing this, we are forever enlivened.

When I write, I'm only trying to reach the River of Light that informs all life and to drink from it, so I can be a conduit for life-force in the world. When I teach, I'm only trying to bring those who are willing to the River of Light, where we can drink and look at each other through awakened eyes. For I firmly believe that all forms of expression and education are meant to awaken the love that is possible in the world.

And so, you don't have to work to find what is lasting and enlightened. You simply have to open your heart and let what's there flow. The rest will follow. Expression will find you. For water finds water, light finds light, feelings find meaning, and love finds love.

The Life of Expression

As no one can live without inhaling and exhaling, no one can live without feeling and expressing. The life of expression is how the heart breathes and how our spirit grows in the life that carries it.

As meditation is an ancient art that deepens our relationship to how we breathe, writing is an ancient art that deepens our relationship to all that matters. And just as the reward for practicing meditation is not that we'll become great breathers but that we'll become clear vessels of life-force, the reward for practicing a personal form of expression is not that we'll become great writers but that such practice will help us wake closer to life.

I want to affirm from the outset that this inquiry into the life of expression is not just about writing but the unnamable process under all art forms—the process of perceiving and feeling our way into life. And more than whatever we might create, the value of inhabiting this timeless process resides in how it helps us come alive by staying in conversation with life. So, while the examples and stories from different fields of creativity help to reveal this process, this book is not just for writers and artists but for anyone intent on staying close to the pulse of life.

As one form of expression, writing, whatever form it takes—poetry, story, memoir, or reflection—is a personal and necessary conversation with the Universe. And while there are many outstanding books that focus on craft and language, this book focuses on the irrepressible aspects of expression, how the forces of life enter us and leave us, and what they do to us on their way through. The exercises throughout are intended to introduce you to the skills of vision, perception, feeling, and articulation, which are the veins and arteries by which Spirit moves between us and the world. Whether we consider ourselves artists or not, we perceive and express as a way to extract what is essential to live.

Retrieving this book has allowed me to shape and share a lifetime of inquiry about the life of expression. It has given me the chance to explore the art and practice of writing as a means to unfold our spiritual growth.

The book began as a popular, two-day intensive workshop offered at the 2013 and 2014 Sounds True Wake Up Festivals. Since then, I have evolved that workshop into this book, which focuses on how bearing witness to the truth of living reveals the mysteries of life. As the journey unfolds, you will be invited to explore the paradox of effort and grace, and to personalize the life-force that comes through the creative process. As you become more familiar with your own voice, you will be introduced to the expressive work of being.

The arc of the book explores how we are constantly being shaped by life into finer instruments of care and expression. The deeper we go, the more attuned we become and the more we join with everything around us. Whether your writing is published or not, whether your music is recorded or not, whether your art is in a gallery or not, whether your garden is given a prize or not, or your cooking is featured in the local paper or not—inhabiting a personal life of expression is its own reward, by which we strengthen our connections and find our way.

The journey of the book is designed to help you personalize the way you take in life in all its varied mystery. Part 1, Basic Human Truths, describes the ongoing relationship between the forces of life and our human nature. Part 2, Being Shaped by Life, shows how these forces of life shape us, refining how we take in experience and how we turn what we experience into acts of care and expression. Part 3, The Deeper We Go, details how we can inhabit a lifelong practice of listening, expressing, and creating. And Part 4, Becoming One With, examines the rhythms of wakefulness and sensitivity that open before us as we get closer and closer to life. Whether you consider yourself an artist or not, the hope, the goal—for you and me—is to wake up to life through our enlivened practice of expression.

I have also discovered that this book is not meant to be read all at once. In writing this book and in reading it, I have found that vast terrains open if you give yourself time with each story, metaphor, and exercise. Therefore, I invite you to enter this book as you would a train traveling across Europe. You can take the express or you can realize that your experience of Europe is really in the stops you make along the way. I invite you to read and consider, then stop and explore the stories and exercises while living your life. For this book is meant to be experienced and journeyed with. When you find yourself speeding up, I encourage you to slow down and live where you are more fully by practicing your own sense of expression with each chapter.

When I speak of poetry, I mean more than the careful arrangement of language on a page. Rather, I mean the authentic life of expression that rises from us when we touch into the depth of life. As John F. Kennedy understood, this serum from underneath our trouble restores us when we've lost our way:

> When power leads [us] towards arrogance, poetry
> reminds [us] of [our] limitations. When power
> narrows the areas of [our] concern, poetry reminds
> [us] of the richness of [our] existence. When
> power corrupts, poetry cleanses, for art establishes
> the basic human truths, which must serve as the
> touchstone of our judgment.

Over the years, I have come upon many basic human truths by way of metaphors and stories. They are quiet teachers that have come to me through listening, writing, and reading. I have tried to sit at their feet and work with them. I assemble many of them here to unfold what I've learned and, in many cases, to pursue what I have yet to learn and to work with them further. While each at the time preoccupied my attention, I see now that they point to one essential theme—the recurrence of images that educate the heart.

For authentic, truthful expressions help us make the journey from our head to our heart. When we can surface without masks and stay in conversation with life, these essential expressions arrive with their wisdom. In this way, I retrieve poems more than create them. They become my guides. They become my inner curriculum. By listening to them, I learn and grow. And when I listen, I'm drawn to what I need to learn.

This way of learning is available to us all as we meet and learn from the moments of our lives. And so, I invite you to perceive and express your way through this book, to write your way through the topics and the stories by way of a journal. To help with this process, I offer "invitations" at the end of each chapter, which include prompts to write and to be in conversation with a friend or loved one. For conversation—the art and practice of truly listening to ourselves and each other—is a restorative mode of reflection. In essence, conversation is an agile and ever-present means of healing that is always very near. If you're not in a place to converse with another, you can have that conversation with yourself, in your journal, on a walk, or at a café.

After all these years, I realize that, when fully present, what matters moves through us the way air moves through an open window. And being such a window is growthful for anyone. For when we practice our own authentic, open form of expression, we all become artists. For any art form or hands-on endeavor, devoted to in earnest, will reveal the same dynamic center at the heart of all expression. However we are drawn into it, the deeper dimension of the creative, expressive process will animate our soul. When moved to drink from the River of Light, we start to glow.

As the sculptor Henry Moore affirmed, "To be an artist is to believe in life." This book is intended to enliven your belief in life. My hope is that this journey will touch into the miraculous depth of being that is always just below whatever you carry, and that you'll return to your life having discovered and deepened a very personal form of expression that you can walk with in your days.

Part 1

Basic Human Truths

The fundamental truth of being human is that we are incredibly sensitive creatures whose joy and pain are registered through that unique sensitivity. This sensitivity allows us the gift of seeing and perceiving. This sensitivity allows us to make sense of being alive. Unlike any other form of life, being human allows us to fit things together or to break things apart.

Inhabiting the art of expressing ourselves is what lets us fit things together rather than break things apart. The art of expressing ourselves—what we experience, what we feel, what we think, and what we imagine exists within us and beyond us—is a form of inner breathing. And so, we each must learn how to do this or we will cease to exist. If you stop breathing, you will die. If you stop expressing, you may still walk around and buy groceries and pay the bills, but you will not be alive.

This lifelong process of weaving what enters us with what rises within us is the necessary art by which we lift the veils between us and keep the world together. As life marks us up, we keep playing the chord in our heart, which echoes the inner experience of truth. We discover, one experience at a time, that a life well lived is well expressed. When most vibrant and vulnerable, we live as a tuning fork, releasing the one conversation that never ends—the conversation of listening, expressing, and creating life.

This part of the book describes the ongoing relationship between the forces of life and our human nature, and the risks necessary to be fully present to whatever comes our way.

Why Write

*Any "discovery" we make about ourselves or the meaning of life
is . . . the coming to conscious recognition of something, which
we really knew all the time, but, because we were unwilling or
unable to formulate it correctly, we did not know we knew.*

W. H. AUDEN

The Thread

Thirty-four years ago, in my mid-thirties, I was working hard at becoming a good poet when I was thrust into my journey with cancer. The torque of that experience pulled me from all my goals and routines and aspirations. I was left in the raw, uncertain simplicity of being alive and trying, by any means possible, to stay alive. I had few native gifts to help me through. The one closest to my heart was the aliveness of expression that lived below my want to be a poet. And so, I began to journal daily about my deepest fears, feelings, pains, and dreams—about the prospects of living and dying. I didn't think of it as "writing" or as "material." More, I was climbing a rope of honest expression, day by day, into tomorrow. It became a muscular and tender, honest space in which I began to access my own inner healing. This was my first in-depth experience of writing as a spiritual practice.

Years later, I read William Stafford's poem "The Way It Is," which I share here:

> There's a thread you follow. It goes among
> things that change. But it doesn't change.
> People wonder about what you are pursuing.
> You have to explain about the thread.
> But it is hard for others to see.
> While you hold it you can't get lost.
> Tragedies happen; people get hurt
> or die; and you suffer and get old.
> Nothing you do can stop time's unfolding.
> You don't ever let go of the thread.

To discover the thread that goes through everything is the main reason to listen, express, and write. Years after this, I learned about the Buddhist myth of Indra's Net, which encircles the Earth. At every knot in the net is a jewel in which you can see all the other jewels and the entire net reflected. This is a metaphor for our part in a living Universe. For each soul is such a jewel, which when clear, will reveal all the other souls in existence as well as the net of being that connects us.

I began to understand that listening, expressing, and writing are the means by which we stay clear, the inner practices by which we realize our connection to other souls and a living Universe. So, to discover the thread that goes through everything is not only how we survive the tumble through life, it is also the way we inhabit our connections. In truth, when we listen, express, or write, we wipe our jewel clean and sustain the threads that hold the world together.

To discover the thread that goes through everything
is the main reason to listen, express, and write.

An Invitation to Follow the Thread

- William Stafford speaks about a thread that goes through everything which we need to follow to recover our well-being. In your journal, begin to describe what stays constant for you, whether you are lifted into joy or thrown into pain or sadness. Over the years, how have you talked about this constancy that you experience and to who? Given all this, how would you describe the thread that runs through everything, as you experience it today?

- Wait a week and discuss the thread, as you know it, with a friend or loved one, asking how the thread appears to them.

The Necessary Art

Each of us is called to listen our way into the underlying truth that connects us all, though we experience this calling as a very personal journey, the way plants and flowers grow and blossom differently, though they all root in the same soil. This rooting and breaking ground until we flower is the necessary art of coming alive.

As Rainer Maria Rilke offered in his legendary *Letters to a Young Poet*: "Go into yourself and test the deeps in which your life takes rise; at its source you will find the answer to the question whether you must create."

I would take this further, because I believe we all must create—that is, we all must root and break ground until we flower. This necessary art of coming alive is not reserved for the few. It is every person's destiny, though there are always things in the way. Not because we're unlucky, but because this is the nature of our time on Earth.

In your mind's eye, imagine a wave building and cresting as it approaches shore, only to have the undertow pull it back out, only to have that returning water gather itself into another wave that will build and crest again on shore. In this way, we are called to gather ourselves in order to come forth into life, and the difficulties—like fear, pain, worry, confusion, and loss—comprise the undertow that pulls us back. Until we can gather ourselves again. And paradoxically, it is the undertow that swells into the majesty of the next wave. This is the human journey.

And poetry is the unexpected utterance of the soul that comes to renew us when we least expect it. More than the manipulation of language, it is the art of embodied perception—a braiding of heart and mind around experience. When a fish inhales water, somehow it mysteriously and miraculously extracts the oxygen from the water. Through its gill, it turns that water into the air by which it breathes. This ongoing inner transformation is poetry. A much deeper process than fooling with words. For us, the heart is our gill and we must move forward into life, like simple fish, or we will die. And the mysterious yet vital way we turn experience into air, the way we extract what keeps us alive—this is the poetry of life that transcends any earthly endeavor. All this while the Universal Ground of Being we call Spirit is working its unknowable physics on us, eroding us to know that we are each other.

As sheet music is meant to be played, poetry is meant to be felt and heard. In this way, what we feel in our depths is poetry waiting to be voiced. And just as music, once heard, stirs our very being, voicing our feelings stirs our consciousness. After all these years, I can affirm that the gift of poetry is how it allows us to be intimate with all things.

In modern times, there are two very strong yet subtle ways that we are darkly conditioned away from our intimacy with life. Both are difficult to shake. One is the manufacturing mindset by which we turn everything into a product: our time, our love, our dreams, our worry, our fear, our art. The other is the way we are taught to place ourselves with authority at the center of all existence. In essence we are taught to play God, to be mini-creators who control everything we come in contact with. This can distort all artists, especially writers.

I have learned over time, after being battered and smoothed by experience after experience, that creativity, whatever form it takes, is less about creating something out of nothing and more about being in relationship and conversation with life and the unknown. The more we engage expression and writing as a way to listen and to stay in relationship with life, the more sacred our path. We are not meant to bend material to our intent, but to bend our will to give voice to life and its rhythms. After my struggles with cancer, I began to learn that what is not ex-pressed is de-pressed. And so, I've become more interested in the expressive journey of healing than creative writing. Ultimately, the purpose of art in all its forms is to make life real, to remove everything that gets in the way, and to help us live.

For each person is born with an unencumbered spot, free of expectation and regret, free of ambition and embarrassment, free of fear and worry; an umbilical spot of grace where we were each first touched by God. It is this spot of grace that issues peace. Psychologists call this spot the Psyche, theologians call it the Soul, Jung calls it the Seat of the Unconscious, Hindu masters call it Atman, Buddhists call it Dharma, Rilke calls it Inwardness, Sufis call it Qalb, and Jesus calls it the Center of Our Love.

To know this spot of inwardness is to know who we are, not by surface markers of identity, not by where we work or what we wear or how we like to be addressed, but by feeling our place in relation to the Infinite and by inhabiting it. This is a hard lifelong task, for the nature of becoming is a constant filming over of where we begin, while the nature of being is a constant erosion of what is not essential. Each of us lives in the midst of this ongoing tension, growing tarnished or covered over, only to be worn back to that incorruptible spot of grace at our core.

When the film is worn through, we have moments of enlightenment, moments of wholeness, moments of *satori* as the Zen sages term it, moments of clear living when inner meets outer, moments of full integrity of being, moments of complete Oneness. And whether the film is a veil of culture, of memory, of mental or religious training, or of trauma or sophistication, the removal of that film and the restoration of that timeless spot of grace is the goal of all therapy and education.

Regardless of subject matter, this is the only thing worth teaching: how to uncover that original center and how to live there once it is restored. We call the filming-over a deadening of heart, and the process of return, whether brought about through suffering or love, is how we unlearn our way back to God.

The purpose of art in all its forms is to make life real, to remove everything that gets in the way, and to help us live.

An Invitation to Listen with Your Heart

- If our heart is our gill, describe an experience that moved through your heart and the one essential thing your heart extracted from this experience that has helped you stay alive.

- In your journal, describe the kinds of things you listen for and give attention to. Are they aspects of nature? Are they pieces of music? Are they stories of certain people in your life?

- In conversation with a friend or loved one, discuss how the nature of how you listen has evolved over the years.

The Unexpected Utterance

For me, poetry is where the soul touches the everyday. It is less about words and more about awakening the sense of aliveness we carry within us. To walk quietly till the miracle in everything speaks is poetry, whether we write it down or not. I confess I started out wanting to write great poems. Then, I was worn by life into wanting to discover true poems that would help me live. Now, in the second half of life, I want to be the poem!

Carl Jung spoke of the poet, and more largely the artist, as a lightning rod for the Unconscious. He held the poet and artist as the conduit through which the collective experience from all time passes. When feeling what is ours to feel, each enlivened soul is a conduit for all of life. In this way everyone, when thoroughly here, is a poet.

In a Jungian sense, I know my truest work has come from beyond me. And I believe that all the great artists, whoever you think they are, would affirm the transience of their genius over the ownership of such gifts. As the Romantic poet Shelley puts it: "Poetry is not like reasoning . . . for the mind in creation is as a fading coal, which some invisible influence, like an inconstant wind, awakens to transitory brightness."

It is our receptiveness to the forces of life that makes us brighten, that makes us a filament for the Mysteries. Another English writer, D. H. Lawrence, affirms this when he says, "Not I but the wind that blows through me."

This doesn't mean that we don't participate or give our all. On the contrary, it is only by giving our all that we open our soul as a conduit to all of life. Whenever we do this, we're sensitive enough for the unexpected utterance to flow through us. Athletes experience this as being "in the zone." The reward for giving their all, through their immense practice and effort, is to enter the flow of the game, the way a fish swims with all its might to catch the current. When our soul is aligned with the current of life, we're often touched deeply by the unexpected utterance of life. And that kiss of the unexpected is often life-changing.

So, what does the unexpected utterance sound like, feel like, look like? No one can know but you. And you will know. When you shovel your walk at night and stop to look at the moon and something in the cold blue makes you realize that there is nothing between you and the heavens, the utterance is speaking to you. When you're bumping through a crowd in Manhattan or Chicago, frustrated because you're late, and suddenly you give up, and in that relaxation of will you realize that there is nothing between you and all the others, and that everyone's heart is beating at the same time—the utterance is tapping you in the chest. When you're fishing and after half a day something bites, and in the tug you're not sure who is catching who, you are in that moment a conduit.

When you breathe fully after the torque of sudden pain or stop crying after being punctured by grief, the unexpected utterance has touched you at the core. And after that recurring fight with your partner, when you fall apart while watching them breathe in their sleep, your love is the utterance. In truth, the inexplicable utterance can appear at any time in any form. It brings us closer to life. It makes us remember that there's nowhere to go.

And when the same red bird seems to be following you, though that seems impossible because you're seeing it in different cities, the unexpected utterance is telling you to stop running. And when the sax player in the second set exhales a soft minor chord that makes it hard to put your mask back on, the unexpected utterance is telling you to stop pretending. And when you hold your father's hand as he's dying and feel *his* father there, the utterance is showing you what outlives us all.

When fully present and working with what we're given, we're compelled by the current of the Mysteries, which informs the heart of our being, the way wind ripples through a lake. When touched deeply enough, we're compelled to make a difference where we live, which is at the heart of our doing. Then, we stop in the rain without thinking to remove a fallen tree that is blocking the road. The novelist David Guterson, author of *Snow Falling on Cedars*, confirms this when he says:

> I write because something inner and unconscious forces me to. That is the first compulsion. The second is one of ethical and moral duty. I feel responsible to tell stories that inspire readers to consider more deeply who they are.

And when the stories weave and knit us together, it is the unexpected utterance that is the thread. So never dismiss the fleeting moments of connection, no matter how they defy ordinary logic. The moment that touches everything is the elixir of the gods, who having to leave this world put all their godliness in that recurring moment.

When feeling what is ours to feel, each enlivened
soul is a conduit for all of life. In this way
everyone, when thoroughly here, is a poet.

An Invitation to Speak Deeply

- In your journal, describe a recent moment when, through the depth of your own feelings, you experienced the feelings of others. Describe how you think this deepening of feeling works.

- In conversation with a friend or loved one, describe a time when you unexpectedly spoke from a deeper place. How did this come about and what came through you?

- Wait a week and, in conversation with a friend or loved one, take the chance to speak deeply about whatever is rising in you or concerning you in that moment.

A Lifelong Process

When the question arises, "Why write? Why create?" I'm drawn to ask, "Why breathe? Why climb to a place where you can see the horizon? Why look for things soft and durable to wrap around a wound? Why call into the canyon between us to see if anyone is there?" Because all these efforts help us live.

Repeatedly, we're called to engage experience as a way to manifest what we carry within us, bringing what is dormant into the world. As the tree that a seed carries breaks ground in time, reflection, dialogue, and writing are seed-like forms by which we release our inwardness into the world. This is why we listen and express. This is why we write, why we create. Because expression is like sunlight that emanates from within. It causes the soul to blossom in time.

Like breathing and waking, expression is a lifelong process that no one can do without. So when you engage in a personal form of expression, you are watering the seeds of your soul. And while fear and pain can keep us hidden, our urge to express and create remains compelling and relentless. Consider the astonishing industry of ants building mounds of dirt hundreds of times their size, and the diligence of bees that can't stop making honey. We are born with the same industry and diligence to create a home and to make honey. We do this to stay alive and to keep the Universe connected and growing.

There are many examples of our irrepressible urge to express and create. Consider the massive expanse of Buddhist temples built in the fifth and sixth centuries in the Shanxi province of China. Known as the Yungang complex, this remarkable set of creations is composed of 252 grottoes with 53 sanctuaries and more than 51,000 Buddha statues.

Some cave temples are small retreats intended for individuals. Others are large compounds with multiple caves filled with sculpted and painted images, as well as living quarters for monks and guests that include libraries and kitchens.

Unlike the Pyramids and the Great Wall of China, which were built by forced labor, the Yungang Grottoes were created by paid labor, largely under the supervision and patronage of Emperor Xiaowen of Northern Wei during the Taihe period (477–499). From space, these grottoes must seem like the most elegant of human anthills.

A more contemporary example of our tireless urge to express is the communal creation of the AIDS Memorial Quilt, conceived in 1985 by Cleve Jones in tribute to San Francisco Supervisor Harvey Milk and Mayor George Moscone who were assassinated in 1978. In time, adding to the Memorial Quilt became a way for those overwhelmed by loss to keep their love alive while stitching their grief together. And the tapestry revealed and strengthened an underlying kinship. After forty years, the Memorial Quilt continues to grow and now consists of more than 48,000 individual panels created by more than 94,000 people. The Quilt, sheltered in a warehouse in Atlanta, weighs close to 54 tons.

On an individual level, we can look with awe to the French Impressionist Camille Pissarro, who pioneered painting outdoors. Ever fascinated with rendering the effects of light, Pissarro created hundreds of landscapes. Or we can look to Claude Monet, who was equally prolific into his eighties. Or to the incomparable Beethoven, who, while going deaf, composed nine symphonies, five piano concertos, thirty-two piano sonatas, sixteen string quartets, and even an opera. There is also John Milton, who dictated *Paradise Lost* to his daughter because he was blind. And the sprawling yet intimate lifelong diary of the great American poet Walt Whitman, which he named *Specimen Days*. This remarkable conversation with life chronicles his years as a volunteer medic in the Civil War, as well as his life as a naturalist and living witness of a maturing if troubled America.

These towering examples are not meant to dwarf our ordinary efforts, but to affirm just how powerful and undeniable the impulse to express and create is. It lives in each of us, waiting for us to engage so it might lighten our burden and enliven our being in beautifully ordinary ways. The way my wife, Susan, extends infinite care in choosing gifts that will speak to the soul of those she loves. The way my friend George cared for his mother in her final days. The way a single mom I know built a tree house for her little boy.

Yet there is a dark busyness that can complicate our urge to express and create. Since the industrial age, we have subverted our creativity as a way to mass-produce a plethora of practical things including cars, trains, planes, weapons, and even—in the noblest sense—as a way to produce art and literature in hopes of achieving something great and lasting. And though the gifts of progress are indisputable, none of our achievements is as important or sustaining as our inborn capacity to come alive, express, and stay connected. It does no good to build a house if there is no one to live in it.

Under all that we build, there is a vibrant sphere of expression that doesn't result in any tangible creation. These efforts lead us to the small transforming epiphanies that clear us out, until the still jewel of a moment at the end of every storm has us blossom into how rare it is to be here at all. This is the quiet and indestructible reward of all introspection, the filament of being that hushes us to bow and help each other up, whether we know each other or not. This hush of simple being is worth all our dreams of achievement.

*This is why we write, why we create. Because
expression is like sunlight that emanates from
within. It causes the soul to blossom in time.*

An Invitation to Know Your Creative Force

- In your journal, describe a creative person you admire
  and an expressive person you admire. What do these
  people have in common? What is unique to each?

- In conversation with a friend or loved one,
  describe your earliest experience of being
  creative or expressive. After this conversation,
  unfold this early experience in writing.

- In your journal, describe a recent time when you felt
  compelled to build or repair something, focusing
  on the moment that energized you to do so. What
  did this feel like? How did it present itself?

Yearning to Be

So, we don't create to achieve or make history, no matter how we're schooled or what we tell ourselves. We create because we have to. And the reward for creating, in any form, is that it keeps us alive. This is why we devote ourselves to art. It is our covenant with life. And like anything we devote ourselves to, we will in time become good at it. But we don't do it to become better. We do it to become whole. For while we can get better without becoming whole, we can't become whole without getting better.

Everywhere we look, life is burgeoning. Plants, trees, and flowers are always pushing up, breaking ground, and yearning to be. Like the seeds of the natural world, there is some innate impulse in each of us to break ground and sprout. But too often the machinery of tradition aberrates this impulse into a compulsion to produce and achieve. And soon, we lose our lifeline to wonder.

Yet, despite the press of our ambitions, excellence is more a by-product of immersion. A dolphin breaches surface to taste the air. It doesn't leap to be an acrobat. So yearn, sprout, and push your heart into the world. Immerse yourself and live. More than accomplished artists, the world needs impassioned creators to dive and break surface.

We create because we have to. This is why we devote ourselves to art. It is our covenant with life.

An Invitation to Walk in Detail

- Take a walk and detail in your journal all the forms of creativity you witness along the way.

- Later, take a walk inwardly and detail the various forms of yearning that you share with all of life.

Lifting Veils

What was any art but a mold in which to imprison for a moment
the shining, elusive element which is life itself—life hurrying
past us and running away, too strong to stop, too sweet to lose.
WILLA CATHER

In my twenties, I lived under a veil of neediness that came
from feeling unworthy. I could never be certain that I was
loved, and so I worked very hard to be indispensable to others,
hoping to make myself needed. Then, I thought, those I cared
about would have to love me. It was almost dying of cancer in
my thirties that ripped the veil of neediness from me. Breathing
in the hospital at night after surgery, I saw the world without
veils. I suddenly heard the others breathing around me. For the
first time, my simple breathing was enough. I didn't have to do
anything to be loved. Suddenly, being human was being a piece
of nature. I doubt if a fish or bird or fox feels unworthy. I was
alive in a quiet way I'd never been aware of.

Since then, I've learned that life covers us with its veils, and
living lifts the veils. And we must remain devoted to the lifting
of veils. The great Hindu poet Rabindranath Tagore points to
how "It is part of a poet's religion to [engage] a solemn faith in
[their] own function, to realize that [they are] specially called to
collaborate with [their] Creator in adding to the joy of existence."

Again, I think this applies to more than poets, for this is
everyone's fate. We all collaborate with the Universe "in adding
to the joy of existence." This is our work in being here. And
when I'm stuck behind yet another veil, when I'm feeling bad
about myself for getting enmeshed one more time, I recall that

unencumbered breath in the hospital that was veil free and declare myself to the Universe, the way a hawk might screech as it leaves a tangle of branches.

The truth is that while I will always be a poet, the way a fish will always be a fish, it has always been so I can know the depth that carries me. Suffering has taught me that an irrepressible cinder of life-force waits in the ruins of every catastrophe as well as in center of every stillness. And we are destined to run about the world until we exhaust ourselves of all striving in order to refind that cinder of life-force, in order to discover what Willa Cather calls "the shining, elusive element which is life itself . . . too sweet to lose."

Repeatedly, we move through our days living in the center of a paradox that has us wake in a world whose outwardness shapes us, while it is our inwardness, through dream and feeling, that fills that shape.

There is a Mayan tale of creation that offers some insight into the purpose of dream:

> It was then that the gods realized they still had not finished their work of creation. In no time these godlike people would tire of being thankful for their lives and for the corn that gave birth to them. And so in one last act of creation, the gods veiled the eyes of the corn people, so that they could no longer see beyond their own time and place. In that one moment the eyes of every living person became clouded, like a valley covered in early morning mist. From then on, the corn people could see only what was near and real.
>
> But as the roots of all living things are one, the gods could not take every bit of magic away from their people. And so the Mayan children and their parents

believe that at night when they go to sleep, the gods lift the veil over their eyes and in their dreams they see deep into the center of the world.

In dreams and in the heart of what we feel, we see deep into the center of the world. Two more reasons that we listen, express, and write are to lift the veils from our eyes and to know the deep. We need to practice these deep arts so we can recover our kinship with all things. This has been the rhythm of life since the beginning: experience covers us, and dreams and feelings uncover us.

In the Hindu tradition, *Maya* refers to the veil of illusion. Hindu scholar M. Hiriyanna describes Maya as "the power [or veil] that conceals the true character of spiritual reality."

Another scholar, Paul Deussen, offers that the great, anonymous Hindu scriptures known as the Upanishads "describe the Universe, and the human experience, as an interplay of Purusha (the eternal, unchanging principles) and Prakriti (the temporary, changing material world). The former manifests itself as Atman (Soul, Self), and the latter as Maya (the veil of illusion)."

A core purpose of dream, feeling, expression, of art itself, is to return us to the ground of the eternal, unchanging principles that we know in our soul carried by a self, no matter the swell and crash of the changing material world. We have no choice but to live in this ever-changing realm, and so the need for introspection and reflection.

Just what kind of veils, then, are we talking about? There are many, but here are a few: the veils of memory, regret, ambition, expectation, fear, woundedness, self-centeredness, and familiarity.

Consider the aging athlete who, having gone lame, sees the entire world through the veil of lameness. Or the insecure executive who feels certain everyone is judging him behind his back, and how he sees the world through a veil of distrust. Or the strong, hidden woman who can't climb out of the canyon of her wound, and how she sees life as an endless climb through wounds. Or the one who is always thirsty, and how she sees the world as never quenching.

At times, the hardest work before us is to part our veil so we can know the deep. And writing is a way to pull a thread and unravel our veil over time.

A core purpose of dream, feeling, expression, of art itself, is to return us to the ground of the eternal, unchanging principles that we know in our soul carried by a self.

An Invitation to Lift a Veil

- In your journal, tell the story of one veil that has lifted from your eyes. It may have been a veil of memory, regret, ambition, expectation, fear, woundedness, self-centeredness, or familiarity. Describe what it felt like to live under that veil and what it feels like to be free of it.

- In conversation with a friend or loved one, describe a veil you are currently struggling to lift and what your next step might be.

- In your journal, create a parable, a small story, about a person who lives under a veil until a dream awakens them to other possibilities.

The Gift of Vision

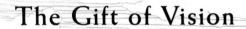

*The arts are the wilderness areas of the imagination surviving,
like national parks, in the midst of civilized minds.*
CLAUDE LÉVI-STRAUSS

What It Means to See

To see takes time like to have a friend takes time.
GEORGIA O'KEEFFE

I was born a seer. Early on, words became the brushes with which I tried to paint what I saw. In time, I learned that while art is movement through space and music is movement through time, poetry is both. And each of us is born with an inclination toward seeing or hearing. I was born a painter and sculptor in a poet's body.

Over the years, I've come across several legendary crossovers in the arts: those whose vision comes in one form while their expression comes in another. Michelangelo's genius came from being a sculptor forced by Pope Julius to paint, forced to compress and express his gift for three dimensions into two dimensions. The result was his masterpiece, the Sistine Chapel ceiling. George Bernard Shaw was a social theorist and critic in a playwright's body. Aldous Huxley was a philosopher in a novelist's body. And Robert Frost was a masterful short story writer, a weaver of potent yarns, born in a rhymer's body.

The insight here is that each needed to express what they saw through the instrument they were given. This dynamic is what gave rise to their genius. I suspect that if George Bernard Shaw had expressed his social ideas in pure social writing, their potency would have been lost.

What, then, does it mean to see? It is how we apprehend reality, how we take in life. An old English proverb says, "The eyes are the window to the soul." The other side of this truth is that the soul is the window to the world. In fact, our capacity to see is more of an inlet, a place of exchange, letting the waters of the world in while letting the waters of the soul out.

More than anything, seeing is about receiving, the way early photographs would receive images from the world, and in the dark they would slowly develop. This is why stillness and quiet allow what we see and receive to develop within us into patterns of insight and understanding. And reflection and expression through writing is a timeless way of developing what we see and receive.

An early seeing for me happened on a Greyhound bus from Boston to upstate New York in my twenties. I was returning to college from a visit with my aunt and uncle. I was lonely and confused by my mystical sense in a pragmatic world. Staring out the window, I began to see the passing fields of trees as subtle, rooted dancers who outlive us. They were swaying to reveal the wind. They were asking for my attention. When I gave it, they began to show me how Spirit moves through us to be seen in the world. Suddenly, I was seeing all the trees swaying at once. I no longer felt alone.

So, the gift of vision is that it brings us insight and company, when we least expect it, if we don't dismiss what we see. One of the strongest distractions from the gift of vision is our insistence on seeing what we're hoping for instead of what is actually there.

I learned this a few years later when I had a dream, an inner form of seeing, in which I was seeking an audience with the great Chinese poet Tu Fu. I searched for him everywhere. I was told he was returning from a long trip. I climbed a nearby mountain and there he was. As I was going up, he was coming down. I wanted to ask him about fame, and greatness, and the mystery of all that can't be seen.

He was returning to the world to find his family. I was awkward and afraid to ask my questions. But looking at me, he read my mind. As he walked by, he touched my shoulder and said, "If you can't see what you're looking for, see what's there. It is enough."

Without another word, he was gone. I stood halfway up the mountain for a long time. At last, I decided to come back and live in the world, a decision that has shaped the rest of my life. This is one of the deepest gifts of vision, that it rearranges us inside, bringing us to the commitment to live in the world. Where else? Then, poetry and art can help us find our way, alone and together.

The gift of vision is that it brings us insight and company when we least expect it, if we don't dismiss what we see.

An Invitation to See

- Upon waking, give your full attention to the presence of light wherever it leads you. It might land on the chrome of the coffee pot or on the edge of the birdfeeder at your window. Be still and let the eyes of your heart open by focusing on this edge of light. Slowly see where and how the early light connects all things. Then, record this experience in as much detail as possible, letting the light offer you its teaching for the day.

- Later, in your journal, describe an earlier moment of seeing that deepened your understanding of how life works. What were you doing or not doing that allowed you to receive this seeing?

- Later still, write a narrative about a person who, through an episode of seeing or not seeing, comes into closer contact with their true nature.

The Origins

In 1994, I was in Montreal wandering through the Botanical Gardens with my dear friend Robert when we happened into an enormous greenhouse of cacti from around the world. These exotic and substantial treelike plants were five to twelve feet high. It could have been an outdoor museum of abstract sculptures. Immediately, I realized that everything we create already exists somewhere in nature as an elemental form.

A few years later, I ran across a recording of hundreds of crickets in a field at night. Magically, when the recording is slowed down, all those crickets rubbing their forewings together sound like a choir in glorious chant. This is more evidence that when we create what we think is new, we recreate fundamental forms that already exist in nature, which have been there since the beginning of time.

With this in mind, we've been miseducated to aspire to do what has never been done. When Ezra Pound said in 1928, "Make it new!" he sparked an entire generation to be as different and avant-garde as possible. But such forced uniqueness has nothing to do with inhabiting the common sense of Origin we all are born with.

Consider Shakespeare, who wasn't original in the Poundian sense at all. His plays were all retellings of ancient histories and folktales. None of his plots were new. Yet what makes Shakespeare so remarkable and enduring is *how* he told these stories. For instance, Amleth was a Roman myth, but Shakespeare gave the story such psychological depth that he rendered the archetypal threshold of individuation that Hamlet faces like no one before or since. In doing so, he portrays the indecisive pocket of heart that each of us carries.

The truth is that we are compelled to rub our wing against the wing of nature until the music of the Universe chants its way through us. The reward for recreating any of the eternal forms is that we invoke the sensation of Oneness, which brings us more alive, whenever we align with the rhythms of life.

It is through our efforts to connect with what is Original, rather than trying to be original, that we resurrect and extend what has always been. For *original* means a return to the Origins. Beyond all craft and technique, this is at the heart of creativity, the enlivening of our deepest nature through our return to the Origins that we all share. It turns out that our yearning to create is less about inventing something new as it is about inhabiting a timeless form, which might be new to us, through which we can feel the presence of all life in all time.

Everything we create already exists somewhere
in nature as an elemental form.

An Invitation to Connect with the Origins

- Take a walk in the city or the country with your journal, and be on the look for original forms in the landscape or the cityscape. Stop and describe the underlying forms that you see. Try to be in conversation with these lasting forms.

- Take a walk in the city or sit in a cafe with your journal, and look at the people around you, trying to see one aspect of their original nature beneath their costumes and roles. Name the original nature you see in each by a gesture such as "hawk gliding" or "dog leaping." In the coming week, weave these gestures into a poem.

- In conversation with a friend or loved one, discuss the nature of being original as it is evolving in you.

The Purpose of Will

As the sun never stops shining no matter the weather, our heart is an inner sun that never stops emanating from within, no matter the psychic or circumstantial weather we encounter in the world. Yet sometimes, when hurt or afraid, we mistakenly shut down as a form of protection, though this only incapacitates us more.

The inner purpose of will is to keep the inner light unblocked and shining, while the outer purpose of will is to open and close the windows and blinds of our life as the weather demands. Our heart is the conduit between Spirit and life. It must never shut down. Expressing what we go through is a major way to keep the inner light unblocked and shining, regardless of what we write or in what form.

Given what it means to see (to be still enough to receive things as they actually are) and what it means to be original (to inhabit presence in a way that returns us to the everlasting forms and rhythms of life), we need a more relational sense of will.

More than controlling events, or shaping material, or setting ourselves apart from those around us, the deeper purpose of will is to move in concert with everything around us, the way a bird glides in wind or a fish swims with the current. The more lasting purpose of will is to join with other life, not to manipulate what comes our way. In this, Einstein was, in my opinion, more of a poet than Picasso.

Both were prodigious talents, but where Einstein worked to pry open the Universe, marveling at what he found in the heart of all things, Picasso was a tireless, if brilliant, manipulator of created forms. And impressive as his sheer output was, it seemed to point more to Picasso than to the creative force he was serving.

While creative spirits like Einstein and Picasso are rare, the thresholds they faced in living are experienced by everyone. It is a spiritual law that we can live one year thirty times, repeating our greatest accomplishments and our worst struggles. Or, if blessed to be forged and shaped by life, we keep growing, until we recognize where we began as the seed of who we have become.

Along the way, we are humbled to discover that we are not gods who carve out rivers, but luminous beings working our way in the stream. Consider the Upanishads, which are the earliest sourcebooks of the Hindu tradition. The Sanskrit word *Upanishad* means a sitting, an instruction at the feet of a master. Since these holy texts are anonymous, the Upanishads have come to be known as instructions at the feet of an unseeable master. All poets and seekers find themselves here eventually: listening at the feet of unseeable masters and recording what passes through, working with what is there to uncover its wisdom.

In staying receptive, we eventually enter the paradox of everlasting will, which requires us to surrender to the unfolding of our heart, in order to discover our true strength. This lasting strength resembles a wave being brought to the surface by the depths of the sea. Each wave opens itself to the sky after being shaped and lifted by the deep. This is why I understand my greatest moments of creative will as those that have shaped me and lifted me into the open.

The deeper purpose of will is to allow us to couple our life-force with other forms of life. Art, then, is the artifact or trail of that holy union. In this way, a flag unfurled completely by the wind is expressing more will than a cowboy herding cattle to their slaughter.

*The more lasting purpose of will is to join with other
life, not to manipulate what comes our way.*

An Invitation to Understand Your Will

* In your journal, describe your earliest memory
  of asserting your personal will and how that
  has affected your use of will as an adult.

* Sit by a river with a friend or loved
  one, and watch the relationship unfold
  between the river and its bank. Then,
  while there, describe what the river
  might say to you about life and what the
  bank might say about being human.

* Later, write a story or poem in the
  voice of the riverbank if it were to
  magically tell its story to a child.

The Unexpected Dimension

In 1514, a young Michelangelo worked hard to sculpt his version of *Christ the Redeemer*. When close to finished, the statue was ruined when he discovered a dark vein running throughout the marble. I think if he had sculpted this later in life, he might have seen the dark vein as an unexpected dimension adding to the statue, not ruining it.

When first learning woodblock carving, I spent weeks carving the reflection of moonlight in a lake. When close to finishing the board, I slipped and chipped off a length in the middle of the scene. I was devastated and thought I'd ruined months of work. My gifted teacher, Mary Brodbeck, kindly put her hand on my shoulder and softly said, "Welcome to woodblock carving." I couldn't help but laugh.

She then said, "Let's do a rubbing of the board and see what it wants to be." With a quiet wonder, she looked at the rubbing and led me into a deeper relationship with the carving, saying, "Remember, where you chipped the board will hold no ink and print as white. So, let's see what other spots in the lake want to be white."

And so, the mistake and ruination of the board became the threshold for bringing the reflection of the moon in the lake to greater life in the print.

My wife, Susan, is a potter. For years, she has participated in Anagama wood-firing, a semiannual, communal process in which fifteen to eighteen potters take shifts raising the temperature of the kiln to 2500 degrees over five days. Then, after a week of cooling, they open the kiln like a tomb to see what the fire has done to their work. Sometimes, the extreme heat will ruin a piece. But more often, the molten ash has scarred and beautified the pots in the most unexpected ways. Sometimes, a platter will be warped or peeled, extending the potter's design beyond what they could have foreseen. Or a vessel will have a crack in it that makes it seem ancient and eternal. The fire has the last word, and the end of all this collective work is to discover and accept what the fire says.

Beyond our most earnest intent, our creative efforts allow us to meet and co-create with life, not bend life to our design. When finally accepting that we relate to material rather than manipulate it, we discover what we create and are changed by the discovery.

In the late 1850s, the sculptor Auguste Rodin started out by renting his first studio, which was a converted horse stable. The young artist couldn't afford to hire models and so paid an elderly handyman, Bibi, to pose, despite his broken nose and weathered face. Over eighteen months, Rodin sculpted the handyman's head, compelled to render the truth of his face rather than turning it into an idealized portrait, which was the trend of his day.

The resulting bust, *Man with the Broken Nose*, was Rodin's first statue of note. The legendary poet Rainer Maria Rilke later wrote about the statue, "There are a thousand voices of torment in this face . . . It does not plead to the world; it carries its justice within itself, [and] holds the [reconciliation] of all its contradictions."

During the coming winter, the back of the statue's head froze and cracked off, shattering on the floor. While distraught and disappointed, Rodin stared at the broken bust and began to see a greater truth in what was left. And so, in 1864, Rodin submitted what remained as a mask to the Paris Salon. It was rejected. But Rodin's experience with Bibi and the shattered bust awakened him to the power of truth over beauty.

Later, Rodin said, "The mask determined all my future work. It was the first good piece of modeling I ever did."

Following what happens over what is intended and working with what-is led Rodin to conclude, "There is nothing ugly in art except that which is without character."

In the expressive journey, regardless of its form, we create more to discover less. In our passion, we create in excess, time and again, so that experience and the deeper elements can break, split, and burn off what is unnecessary, leaving us with only what matters. I don't think I would have discovered the moon's reflection in the woodblock had I not imagined more than what was needed and chipped off that length in the middle of it. I don't think potters would discover the unexpected beauty and warp of their pots without offering their expansive wares to be further molded by the fire. Like Rodin, we are drawn to create all we can, only to stare into the broken pieces until we can see a greater truth emanating in what is left.

Beyond our most earnest intent, our creative efforts allow us to meet and co-create with life, not bend life to our design.

An Invitation to Dream

- In 1555, Michelangelo dreamt of a staircase that he wanted to add to the Laurentian Library in Florence, which he designed but never completed. After he died, others built it. But where did that staircase lead in his dream? Imagine your own mythic staircase. In your journal, describe it and write a story in which you climb that staircase and, despite the obstacles you encounter, you discover where it leads you.

We Relate More Than We Author

*I am very interested in the behavior of art rather
than the achievement of art. I see all the arts as
apprenticeships for the big art of our lives.*
DANCER, POTTER, AND TEACHER PAULUS BERENSOHN

We are not the sole creators of everything we encounter. Everything in the Universe has its own agency. When we assume that we create what we see, we cut ourselves off from the life-force that is larger than us and isolate ourselves from the resources of the Universe. We are not the only living voices, and so creativity and expression are deep ways to relate to and honor other forms of aliveness.

When writing my book *Finding Inner Courage*, I discovered that one way to ask, "What does courage mean?" in Spanish is *"Qué quiere decir el valor?"* This literally translates as "What does courage want to say?" The difference inherent in the Spanish view is that whatever holds meaning is alive and has its own vital authority and, therefore, demands us to be in relationship to it in order to learn its meaning. The American view readies us to apprehend meaning or to create it, while the Spanish view readies us to experience meaning as it already exists. The Spanish view tells us that meaning can only be revealed by listening to the life waiting in the voice of every living thing, and only by staying in relationship to that living voice will we experience meaning in our days.

Even the rules of syntax betray our want to play God and be the sole arbiter of all we encounter. Consider our bias to the active voice over the passive voice. At one point in my book *The Endless Practice* I talk about how a metaphor is seen, like a mountain we come upon. During the editing process, a well-intentioned copyeditor corrected that sentence, wanting me to use the active voice, saying that we see the metaphor. But I believe we don't create the metaphor. Like courage, it exists outside of us and lives independently from our ability to see it. I firmly intend the passive voice here, so that the world in which everything is alive can work its magic on us. In fact, calling this the "passive" voice doesn't accurately describe its qualities, just as the word *irrational* isn't the opposite of *rational, intuitive* is. I would rename the passive voice in language as the receptive voice. This allows for life to have its own agency beyond us. This begins to surface a syntax of being over a syntax of doing.

Over time, I have learned that we discover material. We don't invent it. We uncover and retrieve what we create more than author it. Again, imagine the life of a flag, which doesn't create the wind but brings it alive. So too we. For each of us must accept that the only things worth trying to say are unsayable, though what is sparked by our attempts is love and truth.

Essentially, all expression has two noble intentions: to try to say what is unsayable and to bear witness to what is. John Donne, a metaphysical poet in the Elizabethan age, was one of the first in the West to use metaphor as a way to reveal the connection inherent in all things. His deep bond with his wife, Anne, led him to express his landmark image in his poem, "A Valediction: Forbidding Mourning" (1611). There, he compares the twin legs of an ancient compass (which was an A-shaped instrument for drawing arcs to measure distances) to the connection of their souls, which could never be pulled apart, no matter where life might take them:

If [our souls] be two, they are two so
As stiff twin compasses are two:
Thy soul, the fixed foot, makes no show
To move, but doth, if the other do;

And though it in the center sit,
Yet when the other far doth roam,
It leans, and hearkens after it,
And grows erect, as that comes home.

The potency of language, especially imagery, is to try to make visible what is not easily seen. But when in the realm of what is seen, the potency of language is to wholeheartedly bear witness to what is—no more, no less. This is poignantly demonstrated in a poem written by Pablo Neruda in 1936 during the Spanish Civil War, called "I'm Explaining a Few Things," when he says:

The blood of the children on the sidewalk
is like the blood of children on a sidewalk.

When trying to say what is unsayable, we readily turn to images and metaphors and even stories to tease what is unseen into view. But when the world is starkly before us, then turning to images only distances us from the truth at hand. Then, we are challenged to simply speak of things as they are. Then, "the blood of the children on the sidewalk" is exactly what it is. It must be rendered without any filters.

So, since everything is alive, how do we honor its aliveness and listen for the flow of life-force hidden in the open? No one really knows, but literature is the history of our attempts to say what is unsayable and to bear witness honestly to what is before us.

Perhaps God is an infinite secret hiding in the open waiting for each of us to slow enough to receive what is, at first, unseeable. By doing so, we become conduits of Spirit that continually reunify the Whole. This is how life forms begin: energy moves through particles bringing them together, but it is the openness of the particle that enables the life chain to assemble. And what is the heart but the most transparent particle of being known to humankind?

As the legendary dancer-choreographer Martha Graham says in a letter to Agnes de Mille, "Our one innate task, even when unconscious or unwilling, is to keep the channel open." It is out of such transparency that we are renewed while creating things of value. Such openness requires two things: the risk to be, which asks us to slow to the pace of creation where all things join, and secondly, the courage not just to let what comes up through, but to sing it through. It takes courage to give voice to what we experience, the way a coyote howls: not just out of hunger, but out of a visceral joy at being a part of the infinite secret revealed. In this way, we're angels wrapped in skin and fur, racing through thicket after thicket because we sense what can't be seen all around us.

All expression has two noble intentions: to try to say what is unsayable and to bear witness to what is.

An Invitation to Discover

- In your journal, identify some quality you are struggling with. It might be fear, pain, courage, or vulnerability. In trying to understand what this struggle is all about, ask of your struggle, "What does fear have to say?" or "What does pain have to say?" Listen and record what comes.

- In conversation with a friend or loved one, discuss the difference between discovery and invention. How does your understanding of this affect your relationships?

Keeping the World Together

The role of the poet and the artist is to keep the world together. It is said that in ancient times souls intent on living would reach deep into their wound and bring the fire living there into the light. Then, they would wrestle with it and forge it into a tool that would help us live. In this way, when we do authentic inner work, we're forging tools for others to use. And just as the body needs healthy cells to stay alive, the Universe needs healthy souls to keep going. In this way, when we do authentic inner work, we're sustaining a living Universe. For when we care for the part, we care for the Whole.

Here are two stories that speak to the life-force that exists between all things and how we're born to keep the world together. The first story is told by a member of the Ojibwe tribe, which settled across the Great Lakes region of the United States and Canada. It seems that the Great Spirit had trouble keeping the world together, when a little worm said he could help. Knowing that the secret of life lived in everything, the Great Spirit welcomed the little worm's help. So the Great Spirit said, "Help us, little worm," and the little worm slowly spun its barely seeable silk threads, connecting all of creation with a delicate web. The Great Spirit smiled and Its smile cast a light across the Earth, making the web of connection briefly visible. The Great Spirit marveled at the little worm's industrious gift. For the worm was not clever or brilliant but simply devoted to being and doing what it was put here to do: to inch through the Earth, spinning from its guts a fine thread that holds everything together. And so, the Great Spirit said to the little worm, "You have saved us, little worm, not by being great or bold, but by staying true to your own nature. I will let you live forever."

The little worm was stunned and somewhat frightened. The Great Spirit saw this and said, "Don't you want to live forever?" The little worm inched closer, "Oh Father, I fear so many years if I can't grow." The Great Spirit smiled again at the wisdom of one of Its smallest creatures.

"Very well, little worm, I will only let you *grow* into forever. I will give you the ability to spin this precious thread that connects everything around yourself. And when you can enclose yourself within that web and quiet your urge to inch and squirm away, then you will know the lightness of being that I know." The little worm bowed and began to search for a leaf on which to grow. And this is how the Great Spirit enabled the worm to spin the very first cocoon and from its quietude become the very first butterfly.

The story affirms that everything in Creation is connected and that what holds everything together comes from the humble work of living on Earth, spinning from our guts a fine thread that holds everything together. It tells us that the experience of Eternity is possible if we immerse ourselves firsthand in the barely seeable web of connections.

Humbly, like a little worm, it is in us to work our experience—our pain and frustration and confusion and wonder—into threads of silk. Freely, it is our choice to first connect everything with our experience, then to make a cocoon of those connections, and thirdly to enter that cocoon of experience—the way a Native American sweats in his lodge, the way a yogi holds her third eye, the way a monk maintains his vow of silence. The story tells us that if we still ourselves long enough within the web of all there is, we will eventually come to know the lightness of God's being. Our job, then, is to spin, name, and repair the barely seeable threads that connect everything.

The second story comes from a prose poem written in 1894 by Oscar Wilde, called "The Artist." In the poem, a sculptor is moved to create *The Peace That Abides in Every Moment* in bronze. But there is no more bronze left in the world, except in the image of *The Sorrow That Endures Forever*, which he himself created and set on the tomb of someone he loved. The sculptor is moved to visit the tomb of his lost friend. After reliving their time together, he finally takes the image of sorrow and melts it down in his furnace. And out of the sorrow that endures forever, the sculptor creates the peace that abides in every moment.

Wilde shows us that there is no other way. Minimizing our sorrow, or denying the pain of our journey, or obsessing about the gross indecency of injustice—none of these efforts will bring us peace. Only by putting our sorrow and the pain of our journey into the heart's fire can we melt the sorrow that endures forever to its essential element. Only by meeting life and not running from it can we mold and recast what we've been through into the peace that abides in every moment.

This is profound work which no one knows quite how to do, but do it we must. Our inner destiny is to connect everything in life and to transform sorrow into peace. How, then, do you spin, name, and repair the barely seeable threads that connect everything? And how do you transform the sorrow that endures forever into the peace that abides in every moment?

Just as the body needs healthy cells to stay alive,
the Universe needs healthy souls to keep going.

An Invitation to Surface Your Stories

- In your journal, describe a time when someone in your birth family or family of friends held the family together by being authentic about the struggles they were going through.

- In conversation with a friend or loved one, discuss a sorrow that you carry and what steps you must take to transform this sorrow into a moment of peace.

The Art of Perception

An artist must be able to remain aware of everything around him, but once he finds what he needs [he] must focus like a laser on it. Like a whale swimming through the ocean taking in vast amounts of seawater, then straining out what he needs.

ROMARE BEARDEN

What It Means to Perceive

Poetry is a portal, a means of perception. All art is. And just as we can see the very energy of existence through a microscope, we can see the vibrancy at the center of all life through our heart or our mind, when we are clear of bias and noise. Under all the shaping of words, poetry is the threshold of perception through which we taste the shimmer of Spirit that informs everything.

The word *perceive* and the word *receive* have the same Latin root, *percipere*, which means "to understand," from *per*, which means "entirely," and *capere*, which means "to take." To perceive, then, means "to take things in entirely, completely, in a way that covers us with understanding."

But first, we must put down our screens and filters. Once life enters us, then it is useful to discern what has entered. But often we block the true gift of perception by sorting things before they reach us and touch us.

The gift of perception resides in sustaining our sensitivity to wonder, which means that, while we can always learn from others, we are called to be touched by life directly. We are called to maintain our firsthand experience, which then can be integrated with the experience of others. For true perception takes place below all the values and maps we inherit. The great Indian poet Rabindranath Tagore taught his students not to conform to others but to think freely for themselves. And the profound painter Vincent van Gogh affirmed this when he said, "I dream my painting, and then I paint my dream."

My second book, an epic poem called *Fire Without Witness*, came to me in such a dream of perception, which then took ten years to bring to life. The book centers on Michelangelo's painting of the Sistine Chapel ceiling and how the characters he paints come alive to tell their stories as well. And I confess I didn't have a clue where this was going. I was just following the path of perception as far as I could, trusting that another part of the path would present itself, which it did.

The epic poem showed itself like Ariadne's thread. In 1978, I had finished a manuscript and was going to take a break. As I went to sleep that night I had a vision—I have no idea why; perhaps it was intuition—but it was a vision of Michelangelo pondering the empty ceiling. I thought maybe it was an image I'd use somewhere, so I jotted it down. The next day as I was on my way to a workshop in Schenectady, I realized I had no idea what the ceiling looked like. I'd stared at it in books but hadn't truly *seen* it. I quickly went to the nearest library and pulled out several texts. I spent three hours taking notes, and by the end of the next day, the structure of the entire epic poem was clear in my head.

Six months later, I had written a hundred pages. Then I realized I didn't know enough to continue. But I had written enough that the challenge of the project became clear. A symphony of voices was emerging and I began working more as a conductor than a poet. I could let the voices haphazardly interact or have them echo and counterpoint across the book. That meant I had to plan the journey of the book. That caused me to do *real* research. It took six years before I went back to writing the poem.

During that time, I assembled over four hundred pages of notes and charts and schematics—enough to teach art history. It became clear, as I read all the biographies and different takes on Michelangelo and his time, that history is an eye witness telling an ear witness telling a pen witness. As you get farther from the eye witness, there are just clusters of opinion where the many imaginings of others overlap. And the most exciting challenge is where there isn't any corroboration of incidents. Then, the facts become buoys in a channel, but how you storytell your way from buoy to buoy becomes the terrain of historical fiction.

After all that research, the book had a gravity all its own, and though I was obsessed with it, I could only work on it for three or four weeks at a time. It would beat me up, and I would have to take a break. But it was never an option to stop altogether. I was so far into a deep, mysterious tunnel that the only way out was to find the end of it.

When we let life in, it will guide us and form us. For the rush of perception comes as a gift that will call who we are into being, if we can accept life as our teacher.

After finishing my epic poem and exhausting my out-of-balance creative drive, I was struck down by cancer. In this unexpected tumble, the depth of my perception expanded vastly because of my near-death experience in my thirties. I was rushed by life so fully and harshly that I had no choice but to take in life entirely at a felt level. There, I was ripped free of all the maps I had inherited and covered so thoroughly with understanding that I feared I would drown.

But there was a particular moment of perception that transformed me completely. I had had a bone-marrow sampling and a spinal tap during the same hospital visit. Afterward, I was sent home a bit battered and told to lie still for six to eight hours, because moving before the spinal fluid had a chance to regenerate would cause a migraine. Well, it was hard for me to be still, and every time I moved, I was thrust back down on the couch in pain.

It was as if the force of life was insisting that I be still. When I was, I finally looked out the window to see an apple tree in my front yard. I had seen this tree a hundred times, yet never really looked at it. Now, unable to move without inducing pain, I was forced into a moment of indigenous perception. Seeing the apple tree freshly, it came alive, and I *listened* to the tree for the very first time.

Strange as it was, the apple tree spoke to me, not in words but with a bare presence that said, "When you survive this, there will be no more making things up. When you survive, you will only bear witness to the truth of things as they are."

There is no explaining such a moment of apprehension. You can dismiss it if you want—as some have—as an hallucination due to the medicine or the pain. But I know the truth of that mysterious moment, and it has shaped my life to this day.

I called my experience with the apple tree a moment of "indigenous perception." What do I mean by this? Let me unfold it this way. Taking in the sea completely with our mind allows us to grasp its enormity, while taking in the sea completely with our heart allows us to hear the ancient sea speak. This is the crucial difference between modern perception and indigenous perception.

Modern perception expands our horizon and timeline, while indigenous perception allows us to relate to everything more deeply, as a center of living unto itself. This is what the great Jewish philosopher Martin Buber expanded on in his naming of the I-Thou relationship. When we receive life this thoroughly, everything we encounter appears as a living center unto itself. Then God or Divinity appears in the unrehearsed conversation between living centers. This is another way to understand the gift of perception. It brings to life the conversation between living things.

When forced to be still—when forced to stop thinking and planning and worrying—I apprehended the apple tree as a living center unto itself. Doing so, I was able to *experience* the tree, rather than outline and grasp it with my mind. And, as Buber would say, God spoke through the tree in an unrehearsed moment of conversation with life.

When open to life this thoroughly, perception is the courage to cross the invisible wall between us and life, ten times a day, with no expectation of what we might accomplish. It takes courage because the wall always seems taller and thicker before we take that first step.

But step we must, even if our effort of perception is only for a minute. We must step into the garden of our heart, into the walk with our dog, into the woods for a run, or sit down to journal, or take a shower to let the water of Eternity rush through the showerhead, briefly erasing our fears.

Let one small perception lead to the next, knowing that letting things in completely is traveling as far as going around the world.

When we let life in, it will guide us and form us.
For the rush of perception comes as a gift that will call who
we are into being if we can accept life as our teacher.

An Invitation to Perceive

- In your journal, describe how your interest in something has become a passion. It might be gardening or taking engines apart or collecting stamps or reading about a certain part of history or volunteering at a food kitchen. Describe how your effort has led you to perceive more and more, and how your perception and immersion have changed you. If you have yet to experience this, describe this process as you witness it in a friend or loved one.

- In your journal, describe a moment of indigenous perception, when you related to something or someone as a living center unto itself. Recount the conversation of presence that appeared between you and this piece of life. How have you heard and received this teaching?

- In conversation with a friend or loved one, discuss an area of perception that took time to reach you. Describe how over time you were covered with a greater sense of understanding.

To See One Thing in Another

In Boston, in the early '80s, an old friend lent me a scratchy record. There, I heard this ancient wisdom echoed by a contemporary singer, Lourdes Pita, "Everything in the Universe is interconnected. Within each, it is [all] reflected."

Ever since, I have found testaments to this spiritual fact in nature and biology and art, from every age. In the thirteenth century, the great Zen teacher Dogen suggested that any momentary sense of enlightenment is deeply tied to realizing that each part carries the Whole. Consider his magnificent image of a dewdrop:

> Enlightenment is like the moon reflected in a dewdrop on a blade of grass. The moon does not get wet, nor is the drop of water broken . . . And the whole moon and entire sky are reflected in even one drop of water.

When I was young, I was overwhelmed with so much of life racing through me. I didn't know myself and often felt like a drop of water breaking, always spilling the moon and the sky. Finally, I stopped analyzing and unraveling what I knew to be true and trusted my own direct experience of life. When all alone, with the sun on my face, I felt the miracle of existence in a way that couldn't be broken down or undermined. Building on those irreducible moments, I came to know myself.

Over the past fifty years, I've come to understand that this experience of irreducible moments is what informs the inner life of not just a poet but an artist, and not just an artist but any authentic soul blessed to be completely itself. When able to feel the taproot of existence, we are very close to the common nature that informs all things.

It seems that inner always mirrors outer, and the part always reveals the Whole. Each of us when most ourselves are momentary conduits, lightning rods of the Whole, transmitting the essence of things to one another. And so, art is the expression of experience that reveals the inherent connection between all things.

In my late twenties, I was rowing on a small lake in the Adirondacks. When the breeze settled, I stopped rowing and drifted to the other side. There were no cabins, just banks of broken birch, a few jutting rocks, and the small boat was gently scraping through a patch of lily pads. The sun broke through, and it made me lift one pad without breaking its tether to the bottom. As I turned the wet pad over, I was astonished to discover that the underside resembled a living heart. Its pattern of wet veins seemed an anatomical map of a breathing aorta. And its thin stem disappearing to the bottom seemed its umbilical vein.

This was an affirmation that when we stop to truly look, we always begin to see one thing in another, all things reflected in each. This is the artist's job: to look deep enough and wide enough to find the Universe and its infinite connections reflected in the smallest lily pad barely turned over.

It wasn't long after that moment on the lake that I learned of Monet and Van Gogh and how they saw and painted inner patterns of energy and light. It was the French prime minister, Georges Clemenceau, a friend of Monet's, who characterized him as a human microscope at a time when the actual microscope was being invented. It is compelling that both Monet and Van Gogh were looking so deeply into nature that they stumbled into its very fabric. They seemed to look under the skin of existence, painting the muscle and blood and vein of nature that keeps existence going.

Now, I look for these unexpected mirrors in everything. Now, I believe that all art, and all of what art expresses, is already fully formed somewhere in the very fabric of things—just waiting for us to discover it and express it, the way Dogen's dew drop reveals its reflection of the entire moon. In truth, anything looked at closely enough will reveal the suchness of life that flows through everything.

In this way, all creativity is a discovery of what is already present but otherwise unseeable. The effort to create and express is a communion of inner and outer, of finding the large in the small and the small in the large. Art, in its most authentic expression, is always rejoining the part to the Mystery of the Whole. And once revealed, those patterns are our teachers.

Art is the expression of experience that reveals
the inherent connection between all things.

An Invitation to See One Thing in Another

- Look carefully around you at the simplest things until you begin to see one thing in another. In your journal, describe this parallel in detail, and explore the connection in life these details start to reveal.

- In conversation with a friend or loved one, describe two unrelated objects, people, or experiences that revealed to you something they have in common. Look for a third object, person, or experience that shares this commonality. What do you make of the appearance of such commonality?

The Web of Metaphor

Like an interior form of nature, metaphor exists regardless of whether we see it or not. It is there to be seen the way a vista is seen for the climb, but both the metaphor and the view are there even when we neglect the climb.

After a lifetime of climbing, it's clear that the human form of light is love. And only presence and time can warm love into the open, the way immense sunshine and heat can draw the light within a seed planted in the earth to seek its own nature and somehow break ground. This comparison is a metaphor.

I was born with the ability to see in metaphor. This is how I relate to the living Oneness of things. From the earliest age, the world has spoken to me in this way. The analogous relationship of things has called, not in words, but in a silent language that has somehow shown me, however briefly, the web of connection under everything. This gift is a function of presence. When I am present enough, metaphors appear. They are my teachers. All of my poems are just notes from these teachers. Seeing how things go together sustains me.

The fact that I have lived a life as a poet is a testament to my friendship with metaphor. Along the way, the life of poetry exposed itself as a life of Spirit. This in turn is a testament to my friendship with the connectedness of all things. For metaphor exists to reveal and praise the Oneness of things. Ultimately, it doesn't matter if we write anything down or not. True poetry happens the instant a metaphor is seen. The rest is blessed labor to make the invisible visible.

My own path of listening has led me over time into a conversation with everything—with Mystery, with God or Source, with the rivers of change, with you. As I get older, I long even more for the wisdom and companionship of other living things; to stay in conversation with all I love, with all I admire, with all who have suffered and given of themselves to stay alive and to keep life going. My passion now is to stay as close as possible to the pulse of what is kind and true—to stay in conversation with whatever happens and to experience more and more ways to listen.

Over the years, the trail of these conversations has become the books I write. The further I go, the more of one water they are, as if each book is a different-shaped bucket which I haul to the sea, scooping what I can. This comparison is also a metaphor. Each book I retrieve uncovers some learning that leads to the next inquiry. In this way, each book is a teacher, leading me more deeply into the many ways of being here.

The great Jungian teacher Joseph Campbell offered that metaphor is the primary way to bring into view the Whole of Life. As such, metaphors reveal the connections between things. The assumption inherent in all metaphor is that everything is connected, and the poet's job—and the awakened soul's work—is to reveal, inhabit, and sustain those connections. In time, the web of metaphor offers us a glimpse into the luminous gears of the Universe that keep everything together. For every pattern revealed by a metaphor shows another aspect of how the Universe works.

One of the things I love most about writing is that I don't conceive or think up images or metaphors—I discover them. Metaphors come forward in an unplanned unfolding, like broken-field running in football, or a fast break in basketball, or like a wave of improvised jazz. I lean into some field of feeling or pursue some question, idea, or story, and all of a sudden the effort becomes an unrehearsed discovery of connections, and images and metaphors appear.

We discover metaphors by surrendering our attention and staying in honest conversation with the quiet movements of life as they appear before us. Let me share a recent example.

I was visiting Pine Manor, a retreat center for psychological and spiritual exploration in Lake Elsinore, California, where I teach every year. My good friend Gail Warner founded and directs Pine Manor. She is a wise, old soul. I like to come a day early so that Gail and I can re-enter our lifelong conversation about the mystery of being here.

This time, while driving through the mountains, Gail began to tell me of Hades, the Greek Lord of Death, who surprises us all by pulling a loved one from our midst, dragging them into the Underworld. She shared that when her father died when she was young, her mother was dragged there as well, though she was still walking around and caring for her. Gail wondered now about the presence of Hades in her life and asked, "How was I abducted by grief along the way?"

This is a profound question, because everyone is affected by death. As we were driving, I began to imagine Hades in the valley beside the road waiting underground for the next person he could snatch. I imagined him pulling someone from us into the Underworld, the way he might fist a set of roots and pull the tangle of roots deeper into the earth. And that's when the metaphor appeared. For every time Hades takes someone from us, he pulls the network of relationships connected to that person as well, and the roots of the living are tugged underground.

This metaphor helps us understand the impact of grief on the living. We're all connected, and so we can't help but be pulled toward all that lives under the surface when someone dies. This is why we follow those who die, leaning toward their disappearance. When Hades takes someone we love, we go under too. When someone we love is pulled under by grief, we are not separate from them but part of the tangle of relationships that binds us. And so, we are all pulled in varying degrees when someone dies. Everyone is affected. Now, the question becomes, "How has the pull of your tangle affected you and everyone around you?"

The sun came out to sweep the mountains as we drove on, and Hades seemed to turn away from the light, for now. But by sharing what matters along the way, Gail and I had stumbled onto this metaphor that reveals a truth about a passage that no one can escape.

This is just one example. No matter the subject or pattern, metaphor is to words what light is to objects. As objects make light visible, words make metaphors knowable. In the deepest regard, each of us is a living metaphor, here to expose, reveal, enliven, and inhabit the web of connections that makes up the world. Metaphors make visible the incandescent filaments of being that draw us into the world.

Metaphors reveal the connections between things.
The assumption inherent in all metaphor is that
everything is connected and the poet's job—
and the awakened soul's work—is to reveal,
inhabit, and sustain those connections.

An Invitation to Discover a Metaphor

- Take some time alone, outdoors if possible. Be
  still until you feel a deep presence in you and
  about you. Be present until something in the world
  calls forth your full attention. Give your full
  attention until a pattern in life is revealed. Hold
  the pattern in your heart and mind until what
  is analogous with this pattern is revealed. You
  have now discovered a metaphor. In your journal,
  describe the metaphor in detail and your process
  of discovering it. An example of such a metaphor
  cited above is that no matter the subject or pattern,
  metaphor is to words what light is to objects.

- In conversation with a friend or loved one, discuss
  the metaphor you have discovered and what it
  has shown you about the nature of living.

The Aperture of Intuition

The opposite of rational is not irrational but intuitive. And while the mind and heart work together, my experience is that the heart absorbs and integrates more deeply than the mind. One way to think of intuition is as an aperture that opens and closes the heart like the lens of a camera, letting in life until it colors our soul.

Reason is often an intermediary for a quicker, deeper, more elusive facility. Reason allows us to think like a ladder, while intuition allows us to think like a constellation. Weaving both, I write about what I need to know, not what I already know. If I had only written about what I know all these years, I would have written very little.

The truth is that I feel things more quickly and more deeply than I understand them. I understand things more quickly and deeply than I can speak them. And I speak things more quickly and deeply than I can write them. One of the reasons I am so prolific is that years ago I gave up the notion that I had to understand what I was feeling, thinking, speaking, or writing before I could put it down. Since that time, my writing has become an ongoing curriculum, because I no longer record what I understand but explore what I feel. I write because I have questions, and often the writing leads to more questions, not answers. But in the process of expressing, something happens that's valuable to the act of living. And in the same way that a flame gives off heat, I believe that if my expressive search is clear enough and authentic enough, chances are the heat of that fire will warm others.

I've been asked if intuition is Divinely inspired. I wholeheartedly say yes, but I want to enlarge "Divine" to include the Taoist notion that the world is informed by an elusive and incomprehensible yet all-powerful current or life-force, whether we call that current God or something else. Lao Tzu says, "Find the current and things will become clear, the way running water cleanses a rock." The act of living produces oxidation, tarnish, and moss, all of which cover the rock. But like water running over us, the act of feeling, perceiving, and expressing cleans us off. When the rock that is me is clean, I'm most open to the current around me.

Intuition appears when we get out of the way. The mind tries to measure, weigh, and discern things that are beyond its capacity to measure, weigh, and discern. So, there are times when we have to suspend the mind's want to measure what it meets. In order to eat, we have to chew our food to make it small enough to digest. But once that's done, it in no way resembles what we took in. The challenge—spiritually, emotionally, and mentally—is not to make everything we take in assume our shape in order to enter us. But to find ways to open up, so we can take in things as they are and therefore be affected by them.

I write because I have questions, and often the writing leads to more questions, not answers. But in the process of expressing, something happens that's valuable to the act of living.

An Invitation to be Intuitive

- If intuition is an aperture that opens and closes the heart, practice opening your heart by leaning toward whatever is before you and holding nothing back. Close your eyes and hands when you inhale, and open your eyes and hands when you exhale. Repeat this slowly. Once you feel your heart opening, go to your journal and record what comes into you in this moment without preference or judgment. Later, look at what has arrived, and shape what's there into an expression without labeling it as a poem or story or reflection. Simply let it have its own structure and voice.

- In conversation with a friend or loved one, discuss the difference in how you reason and how you intuit, how thoughts come to you and how they affect you, as well as how intuitions come to you and how they affect you. Which is more natural to you, reasoning or intuition? How can you strengthen the one you struggle with?

Releasing the Divine

There are two beautiful notions that speak to our innate yearning to release and be released by the Divine. What I mean by the Divine is the inherent quality of Spirit that informs everything in life.

One notion that speaks to the uncovering of the Divine is Michelangelo's sense that the statue is already in the stone and that rather than create the statue, our task is to figure out a way to release it. The legendary sculptor would carve away the excess marble to reveal the statue already waiting in the block of uncut stone, as if he were freeing a prisoner from a deep sleep. Giorgio Vasari, the biographer of so many Renaissance artists, compared Michelangelo's sculpting process to someone pulling a beautiful form from underwater. The form is complete but out of view until lifted into the world.

What's powerful here is that this is what life does to us. Experience carves away all that is not essential from us until, like Michelangelo's statues, we are released from our sleep and lifted into the world.

Another notion that speaks to the transference of the Divine is Carl Jung's sense of the poet as a conduit for the collective unconscious, which I mentioned earlier. Jung sees the poet and the artist as a lightning rod for the aggregate of dreams, memories, and experiences of humanity, which come alive through the thoroughly personal story of the creative individual.

These two notions imply that everything already exists. For instance, you could look at the same patch of sea a hundred times. But one day when the light is right and you're tired enough, you look at the rise and swell of the waves and it says something to you, something that parallels what's growing or not growing inside you. Now, did the sea suddenly emanate more meaning? No. The world is steadily infusing us with the Divine, depending on the level of our openness.

As human beings, we are a beautiful braid of the infinite and the finite. While our being is bottomless, our humanness has limits. That's the curse-blessing that has us looking everywhere for what's right before us and within us.

In time, we discover that everything carries the Divine. It's all here, waiting quietly in the open to be manifest by nothing less than the complete surrender of our attention and care. As a young poet, I was always on the look for things to write about, concerned with how to manipulate and squeeze content or context out of any circumstance. But gradually, I came to a place where, if I opened myself authentically, something arose from my center, which I term *voice*. I began to realize that it's not about searching for things to write about, but releasing the Divine that waits in everything. It doesn't matter what we write about. If we bring our full being to whatever is before us, the Divine carried in the things of the world will reveal itself through us.

Releasing the numinous quality of Spirit that informs everything through our creativity and expression is the way of all art, which leads us to the purpose of all art, which is to enliven our inherent kinship with all things.

Experience carves away all that is not essential from us until, like Michelangelo's statues, we are released from our sleep and lifted into the world.

An Invitation to Sculpt with Words

- In your journal, experiment with Michelangelo's sculpting process by working with the blank page. Instead of aiming or planning to write something, imagine that a poem or story or passage is waiting fully formed in the blank page, waiting for you to release it. Now be still and quiet until you begin a conversation with the blank page. Begin to lift the already written piece into view, a word and phrase at a time. See what happens.

The Craft of Perception

The aim of art is not to represent the outward
appearance of things, but their inward significance.
ARISTOTLE

Jennifer Blessing, a curator at the Guggenheim Museum in New York City, has said that "Artists pursue various methods of liberating the mind in order to access the marvelous." We are all looking for ways to widen our lens of perception so that we can be more alive. The Black Mountain poet Robert Creeley declared in the 1950s that form follows content. And so we keep searching for forms of expression that will open and liberate the confines of our mind, so we can access and inhabit the marvelous. What we do to find the form that keeps us close to life constitutes the craft of perception.

For me, the craft of perception has led to an all-inclusive form that uses the genres as various tools in one big toolbox. While each genre is worthy of a lifetime's devotion, I have been led to use each as needed in whatever I'm writing, no matter what I'm exploring or expressing. So, all my work is poetry, whether in stanzas or paragraphs, because all my work seeks to express the truth of life through the filter of my heart. And all my work is personal memoir, because the lens of the "I" is the only window we have on life. And all my work is anthropology, because the world is always more than just me. If I need to do research while describing the patterns of life, then I pursue scholarship. If I need to unfold the story of another's life along the way, then I include biography. If I need to illustrate an insight in the form of a story, then I rely on fiction. And if I'm led to weave ideas, then I venture into philosophy. But it all merges into one vibrant, seamless form, which I have no name for.

Each of us must find the one form that will welcome the questions that will liberate our mind. That form and the path to that form may look different for everyone. But there is one practice that can help us find our form. That is the practice of honoring. For the word *honor* means "to keep what is true in view."

To keep what is true in view is an ethic to live by. When I honor you as a friend, I keep what I know to be true about you in view, especially when you can't honor yourself. When I honor myself, I keep what I know to be true about my soul in view, especially when I am troubled or feeling lost. When I honor the lineage of my ancestors, I keep what I know to be true about all those lives which have made my life possible. Keeping what is true in view is a steadfast way to expand our perception and liberate our mind.

So what question is opening you? What form are you searching for that will liberate your mind? And how can you better honor your soul by keeping what you know to be true in view? Entering these questions is the beginning of your personal craft of perception.

Another important ethic to live by and write by is the marriage of truth and kindness. In graduate school, I found myself in the era of the workshop, in which a tough skin was required if you were to be taken seriously. Workshops were brutal and often bloody conversations in which teachers and peers would impose preference as truth and dispense their judgments harshly. What I've come to believe firmly and wholeheartedly is that truth and kindness are not mutually exclusive. There is no reason that truth can't be offered accurately with love. Feedback does not have to be served with a knife.

Furthermore, truthful feedback about writing does not consist of bending an apprentice to the style or form of their teacher. The teacher's job is to help the apprentice develop their own form of expression, be thoroughly themselves, and practice keeping what they know to be true in view. This is how a teacher honors their students.

Toward this end, I offer a few covenants around which to meet, whether in a classroom or a living room:

- Insure confidentiality.

- Invite everyone to listen to each other's work with the aim of helping each person say what it is they have to say in the clearest way possible. This is different than steering people to write the way you do.

- Be specific in writing and feedback. It does one little good to say, "This is great" or "This is terrible." Rather, "This works for me because . . ." or "This doesn't work for me because . . ."

- Encourage each other to view writing as discovery and retrieval, like fishing up something from the deep, rather than invention or creating something out of nothing.

- Encourage each other to view writing as a way to be in relationship with deep and life-giving material, as opposed to authoring and mastering material.

- Invite everyone to read their work aloud and to share how they have been deepened, broadened, or changed for retrieving it and expressing it.

- Enter writing experiences together, not just feedback sessions. For example, invite everyone to write to music at the same time. Or have everyone go to an art exhibit together in silence and write in response to it. Or invite everyone to bring and read a poem (someone else's) that has been significant to them and to share why.

The writer Raj Gill said, "When I say to myself *I know*, I rob myself of the now." And shutting down the now closes our window to life. The first commitment to our craft of perception is to keep our window to life open. The second commitment is to honor our own journey by keeping what we know to be true in view. The third commitment is to offer truth with kindness so that we can meet life and grow.

But the fourth commitment is harder to put into words. It involves keeping our heart open while tumbling through experience. The poet and Jungian analyst Clarissa Pinkola Estés offers this guidance:

How to Write a Poem

Climb to the top of the tallest tree.

Step onto the branch you fear
will break beneath your weight.

Let it break.

Write your poem before
you reach the ground.

The craft of perception isn't entered just to see, but to help us better express what we see, so we can learn from that expression and live more fully.

Each of us must find the one form that will welcome the questions that will liberate our mind.

An Invitation to Keep What Is True in View

- In your journal, identify one thing you know to be true, and tell your history of trying to honor that truth, describing your efforts to keep that truth in view.

- In conversation with a friend or loved one, discuss your own experience of the four commitments of perception: keeping your window to life open, keeping what you know to be true in view, offering truth with kindness, and keeping your heart open while tumbling through experience.

The Chord in Our Heart

Art is the passing of feelings from one human heart to another.

LEO TOLSTOY

As a Tuning Fork

*An artist listens to a song in the heart
and creates from that.*
ROBERT HENRI

From the moment we are born, life begins to carve us into an instrument. How we're carved by experience and how living puts us in touch with the common, eternal chord that rings at the bottom of every heart is what the chapters in this section explore. I begin with my own journey.

I started writing in high school after my first love dumped me. I was devastated. Though I wasn't a loner, I didn't have any close friends—not yet. So I started talking to myself as a way to heal. Once on the mend, I realized I wasn't just talking to myself. I had begun a conversation with the Universe.

As an undergraduate, I was discouraged from writing creatively in the English department. But a kind theater professor, Doc Palmer, took me under his wing and told me that if I became a theatre major, he would take care of me. I began by writing plays; that was part of our agreement. I'd sign up for his courses, though he'd give me different assignments. Instead of a paper on *Oedipus Rex* or *Hedda Gabler*, he'd invite me to write specific scenes modeled after the great playwrights. I also had to partake in every aspect of theater from set design to acting. This unexpected apprenticeship has stayed with me.

Two inherent lessons from theater inform all my writing. First, the theater axiom: show don't tell, by which we give the evidence of an experience, not our conclusion of it. And secondly the very premise of all theater, whereby the play, physically and emotionally, stands naked between the playwright and the audience. Where intellectual writing can cover the work or keep it at a distance or even hold it behind the author, this can't be done with plays, or it isn't a play. These theater principles are in the bones of all my work, regardless of the form. I think my writing is more accessible and better for it.

Yet I did have a moment of epiphany in which I knew I was a poet, though I'd written very little. As a nineteen-year-old, I was coming off the top of a hill in Cortland, New York. I was heading toward the college town below, when a wind rushed at the back of my head and off my cheeks into the space before me. I stopped and watched it gust across the valley, watched as the same clear wind swept through the trees on the distant hill. Somehow, in that moment, in an intuitive way that defied logic, I knew I was a poet. I think I understood the reach.

Early on, I realized that being a poet was mostly about being an awake human being, which in turn was mostly about living each day as a tuning fork in the midst of life's currents. As a young poet, I would stumble into a vision, or trip into a metaphor, or glimpse a truth, or be stopped by a deep question. Then, I'd reach for expression after expression in an effort to capture each of them. Of course, I'd inevitably miss because the only things worth saying are unsayable.

So I'd try again and miss again. I would get frustrated and press myself, trying to capture the original vision five, six, seven times. Why couldn't I express what I was seeing and feeling? Why was I always missing? These things were so clear to me, and yet I couldn't render them accurately. What was I doing wrong?

Now, years after cancer, I've been forced to accept the inevitable refraction of expression that can only approximate the ineffable. This has led me to thank the unsayable for bestowing me with these five, six, or seven attempts, poems that I never would have retrieved if not for the glow of what can't be said. Now I say with gratitude, "Look what the unsayable has given me. It has squeezed these precious drops of insight through me into being."

Now I accept that the original vision is never meant to be captured but is a shimmering conduit through which we can only retrieve expressions that might point to all that is unsayable, that might reveal all the ways we're connected, that might pay tribute to the web of essence that informs existence.

Along the way, I came to understand that the tuning fork is our heart. And letting life strike the chord in our heart helps to alleviate our suffering and inner sense of burden.

The Hindu poet Rabindranath Tagore conveys this beautifully using the image of an Indian instrument known as a *veena*, which is like a sitar:

> I am in search of a veena player. I have tried East and I have tried West, but have not found the [player] of my quest. They are all experts, they can make the strings resound to a degree, they command high prices, but for all their wonderful execution they can strike no chord in the heart. At last I come across one whose very first notes melt away my sense of oppression within. In [this playing] is the fire of joy, which can light up all other hearts by its touch.

When the chord in our heart is struck, we resonate with all living things and with the resources that sustain the Universe. When we give ourselves over to the epic sharing of truth and tenderness that arise from that resonance, it becomes so much more than writing. It opens a window into the Mystery, which shows itself ever so briefly after so much human toil to open that window. To open in this way requires us to be honest, accepting, and loving. Through such courage, we can remove the veils that cover us, long enough to stir our hearts into wakefulness.

In AD 905, the Japanese Emperor Daigo commissioned the first imperial anthology of poetry, known as the *Kokinshu*. When it was completed in AD 920, one of the poet-editors, Ki no Tsurayuki, wrote an introduction that has become one of the most reliable descriptions of poetry and the effort to make meaning of our experience. It speaks to the chord in our heart, which when struck lets us know we are alive:

> Poetry in Japan begins with the human heart as its seed
> and myriad words as its leaves. It arises when people are
> inspired by what they see and hear to give voice to the
> feelings that come forth from the multitude of events
> in their lives. The singing of warblers in the blossoms,
> the voices of frogs in the ponds, these all teach us
> that every creature on Earth sings. It is this song that
> effortlessly moves Heaven and Earth, evokes emotions
> from invisible gods and spirits, harmonizes the relations
> of men and women, and makes serene the hearts of
> brave warriors.

Twenty-two years ago, I began *The Book of Awakening* when freshly on the other side of cancer, as a way to give back by trying to strike the chord in our heart, by trying to offer small doses of what matters for people tangled in the majesty of living—struggling, loving, and dying. My hope was to provide a form of inner food.

I was amazed at how the daybook had been a pliable and thoroughly used form in many lay communities: in cancer rooms, recovery rooms, and support groups. I saw daybooks bent and folded everywhere: in the back seats of cars, left on park benches, and on countless bed stands. I thought if I could fill this form, I might create something of use.

It took two years to gather all the entries and another year to imagine the meditations. And one more year to order the entries and revise them. Then the book began its way in the world.

Since that time, I've come to believe that the heart of awakening is the quietly courageous act of feeling what is ours to feel and facing what is ours to face. And I've discovered along the way that writing—expressing—is one of the best ways to stay awake. It doesn't matter how "good" our expressions are but that they keep us in relationship to the larger Universe we are a part of.

When the chord in our heart is struck, we resonate with all living things and with the resources that sustain the Universe.

An Invitation to Go Below Your Conclusions

- In your journal, identify one understanding or conclusion about life that you feel strongly about. Now describe the experiences that led you to this understanding or conclusion.

- In conversation with a friend or loved one, tell the story of what experiences led you to the understanding or conclusion you wrote about in your journal—without voicing your understanding or conclusion. Once you've shared the evidence of your experience, ask your friend or loved one to offer their understanding or conclusion about what you shared.

The Inner Experience of Truth

Educating the mind without educating the heart
is no education at all.
ARISTOTLE

I have always felt most alive when telling the truth, when the sudden utterance from within—be it a question or a feeling—rings through the entirety of me. And though I've been trained to focus on the objective rewards of truth, such as insight and understanding, I realize now in my sixties that it is really the *experience* of truth—the empowerment of the authentic—that has kept me going.

While uttering the truth or questioning the truth, an electricity is turned on that connects us to that immeasurable vastness so close but always out of view. When experiencing truth, especially the truth of feeling, I feel most like a dolphin breaking surface only to dive. The affirming thing about such moments is that they are wonderfully contagious. In a room full of skeptics, one truthful utterance can shift the entire ground of dialogue, even if no one else dares to say a word.

As a young man, I had no idea of any of this, any more than a hawk is aware of its aerodynamics. Now, I can see that this desire not to be alone in truth-seeking and truth-speaking is what made me want to be a teacher.

I really didn't want to talk about anything outside of truth. I wanted to examine everything by sharing, reflecting, and questioning whatever I would meet through the lens of authentic feeling.

With the exception of a few friends, I couldn't find such companionship readily in the world, and so, without realizing it, I began to write and teach in order to create a sacred place where the experience of honest truth could happen. This very quickly necessitated my introducing my students to the vastness out of view and to their own experience of authentic feeling, so we could enter this sacred place together.

I've also learned that each time we experience truth—each time we suffer or love—the range of our compassion widens. Like a mud-filled pipe that is hollowed out by rain to carry water underground, the force of each experience clears us out. Listening, expressing, and writing are conscious ways to clear ourselves out and to expose and extend the range of what we feel. And so, the poet or artist in us is that deep part of who we are that keeps extending the range of our compassion.

Throughout history, those afraid of the life of feelings have undermined their power and dismissed their rightful role in experiencing truth. For much of my life, I've been called a Romantic, which is true, but not complete. It's like defining the sea by its surface. *Romantic* is a term that has been diminished through the years. Today, it denotes a sentimental outlook on life fueled by unwarranted optimism. At heart, though, it has always been an outlook that assumes there's something larger than the individual. All the energy surrounding such a view arises from a belief in the interconnectedness of all Life and the experience of Wholeness.

At its core, Romanticism suggests that we can become whole through inwardness, by feeling and inhabiting our "inscape," as Gerard Manley Hopkins calls it. "Feeling is all," as the German poet Goethe says.

I would suggest that a mature Romantic is someone who accepts the hard realities of life as well as the unseen connections that knit all aspects of reality together. The great Polish poet Czeslaw Milosz was, in my view, a mature Romantic. He was accurate and realistic about the terrible hardships he experienced and witnessed growing up during the Holocaust. Yet, from under all that, even in his darkest poems, there is a light emanating, informed by something larger than what any one individual can go through or bear witness to. This is what a mature Romantic commits to: a devotion to the truth of living while never diminishing or giving up on the majesty of life that holds that messy turbulence of truth.

I am deeply Romantic in that I believe feelings are the threshold to Spirit. I also believe deeply in the act of expressing and how it helps us move toward being whole and complete. In our experience of truth, perceiving, feeling, thinking, and expressing are all parts of a lifelong process that is equivalent to inhaling and exhaling.

Some of us develop our abilities to feel, see, and hear more deeply than others, though I believe we are all born with the same capacities. Some of us are distracted by the noise of the world—even hypnotized by it—while some of us are tossed below the noise, hearing frequencies the rest of us have yet to access.

Consider how dogs hear well beyond the range of human hearing. In California, it's been reported that dogs have heard the beginnings of earthquakes before seismographs could register their initial tremor. In just this way, there are those of us whose ability to feel, see, and hear is beyond our normal range of compassion. We call them empaths or psychics. And we often discredit them because what they know appears to be beyond what we can sense.

The poet in us is not only committed to the deepest form of feeling, seeing, and hearing, but also committed to learning from those who feel, see, and hear more deeply.

Let me share a story about this deeper kind of hearing. A dear friend emailed me one day in winter from a beach halfway around the world. She ended by asking what my definition of poetry was. It was early. I was at my desk. The house was quiet and I looked at the iced-over trees I know so well. I was touched that she would ask and wasn't sure how to put into words something so essential and invisible that I have devoted my life to uncovering it. Yet this unnamable quest is poetry. How friends search for truth across the miles and years is poetry. How we discover truth through our ongoing conversation together is poetry.

After consulting the trees, I wandered my way through a cup of tea to this poem that I sent her:

You Ask About Poetry

You ask from an island so far away
it remains unspoiled. To walk quietly
till the miracle in everything speaks
is poetry. You want to look for poetry
in your soul and in everyday life, as you
search for stones on the beach. Four
thousand miles away, as the sun ices
the snow, I smile. For in this moment,
you are the poem. After years of looking,
I can only say that searching for
small things worn by the deep is
the art of poetry. But listening
to what they say is the poem.

Months later, my friend wrote me again:

I'm in the South Pacific as I write, watching the waves break gently onshore. I think of each of us as a ripple in the sea that is life. We believe we're all so different, but we're not. We cover ourselves in customs and costumes of aspiration, struggle and victory, sacrifice, and loss—and soon forget who we really are. Lately I've been asking God: Please show me who I really am, [because] I want to make sure I never lose sight of the truth of my existence. I am a ripple in the ocean of God, and I want to be able to see my reflection in the face of everyone I meet, to understand that even people I will never know are reflections of my undisguised self.

We are, at once, individuals and ripples in the sea that is life. And the want to know who we really are and to know the truth of our existence are, to me, the fundamental life-giving questions that the heart commits to once opened by love or suffering.

This all makes me want to share a small ritual I do every time I finish swimming. I slip into a smaller therapy pool filled with warm water, float on my back and, with my arms spread and my ears submerged so I can hear my own breathing, I softly recite this small poem of mine:

My Life

I am a fish
in search of bottom
when I surface
in search of surface
when I bottom
and the ribbon of God's sea

passing through my gills
is what I feel, and think,
and speak.

I think the work of all poetry is to have us live on the inside of truth, so we can accept that everything is alive. The gift of all poetry is to listen to what everything has to say.

*Each time we experience truth—each time we suffer
or love—the range of our compassion widens.*

An Invitation to Explore Your Personal Relationship with Truth

- In your journal, describe who you explore your experience of truth with. What qualities or conditions make that sacred place between you possible?

- In conversation with a friend or loved one, tell the story of a moment in which you felt both the harshness of reality as well as the unfaltering presence of life-force below the situation. Then go back to your journal and, through metaphor or story, explore the relationship between the harshness of reality and the unfaltering presence of life-force that never goes away.

Life Marks Us Up

I was stranded in Washington, DC, due to a storm in Chicago. It was sunny and cold, and I wandered into the National Gallery of Art just beyond the Capitol. On the ground floor in the west building in two small rooms was an exhibit called *In the Dark Room*, which mounted examples of the early process by which photographs were developed in the 1800s.

We don't see many darkrooms any more, given the ease of digital cameras. But darkrooms still offer a small, reflective solitude for serious photographers. The great photographer Ansel Adams had a very elaborate, expansive darkroom, while the Civil War photographer Timothy O'Sullivan refitted an ambulance wagon into his portable darkroom. Progress doesn't limit our toolbox but adds to it, the way that master woodworkers don't throw away their hand tools just because they have a set of power tools.

Essentially, the darkroom process involves surfacing an image already recorded on a piece of photographic paper by immersing the paper in some form of developer. After a time, exposing the paper to light and a developer causes the image to show itself. Before the image is overexposed, the development of the image is stopped by a chemical bath. Then the image, now visible on the paper, is set with a photographic fixer. During the development of the print, reducing the amount of light that is cast on an image is known as "dodging" a print. Letting excess light expose an image further is known as "burning" a print.

In the small gallery, I was staring into this ethereal image of a nineteenth-century horse grazing in a field, when I began to see that this early method of surfacing photographs is, in some deep ways, analogous to how experience leaves its imprint on us. Life marks us up way inside, and when we can hold those markings truthfully, understandings develop in the skin of our heart.

Unpacking what we've been through in the solitude of our reflection—this is our darkroom. This is where we incubate our attempts at understanding until they are exposed, developed, and fixed as glimpses of truth and wisdom. And yet, when we hold back on developing what we know, we dodge the lesson waiting to be revealed. And when we overthink, through worry or doubt, the insight waiting to develop within us, we are burning our experience beyond recognition.

Despite the speed of our age, we need to take experience into our heart and wait for the images of life to show themselves, all of which takes time. And any ounce of honest writing requires the courage to let the lessons of life leave their markings on us. In this way, the practice of listening and reflecting etches its insights into our consciousness, and expression then develops those images into stories or poems. The ounce of wisdom we offer is always the result of the slow internalization of what life does to us.

Life marks us up way inside, and when we can hold those markings truthfully, understandings develop in the skin of our heart.

An Invitation to Retrieve a Lesson from Your Heart

- In your journal, describe one experience that has left a mark on your heart, and hold it long enough in silence that its lesson begins to show, the way a print in a darkroom will in time reveal its image. Describe what this process feels like and what the lesson is.

Feelings Are Paints

Poetry is awareness heightened to the point of love.
PAUL ROCHE

D ario Robleto is a leading conceptual artist whose work is comprised of meticulous reconstructions of fragments of historical objects. Born in San Antonio, Texas, in 1972, his work keeps things alive in a way that always points to something larger. This is the mystical goal of all art.

Robleto's installations are referred to as symbolic displays that mirror the world. He uses the stuff of history as both his medium and as collective evidence of the ways that we hurt each other and help each other. Such felt specificity is a great model for any writer.

The materials he draws on range from rose petals to pulverized human bone to gunpowder found on a Civil War battlefield. The fragments he draws on evoke a presence that questions what we've done while affirming the spiritual dust that binds us.

A powerful example is Robleto's piece *A Defeated Soldier Wishes to Walk His Daughter Down the Wedding Aisle* (2004). In an open space, a worn pair of knee-high boots stands in a swath of sand shoveled across the floor. In the right boot is the remnant of a wooden and iron leg, obviously an early prosthetic. The shuffle-marks across the sand show the weighty journey this soldier had, just to move a few feet closer to what he loved.

Robleto lists his materials as:

A cast of a hand-carved wooden and iron leg that a wounded Civil War soldier constructed for himself.

The replica is made from a melted vinyl record
of the Shirelles's "Soldier Boy" and femur-bone
dust. The replica is fitted inside a pair of WWI
military cavalry boots made from a melted vinyl
record of Skeeter Davis's "The End of the World."
There is also an oil can filled with a homemade
tincture comprised of gun oil, rose oil, bacteria
cultured from the grooves of Negro prison songs
and prison-choir records, wormwood, goldenrod,
aloe juice, resurrection plant, Apothecary's Rose,
and bugleweed. The remaining elements of the
installation are brass, rust, dirt from various
battlefields, ballistic gelatin, white rose petals,
and white rice.

Combining remnants in this way can jar our sense of the past
until we realize that everything keeps living. Work like this
compels us to feel and mix the voices of those in prison singing
their songs with the hands of those pressing the records, and the
blood that dried in the dirt from those battlefields with the pollen
of a resurrection plant, and the bone dust from soldiers long gone
with torn boots worn in war, until all that suffering is ground with
the pestle of art into the mortar of our consciousness—all this
at once.

To single out a wooden and iron leg that a wounded Civil War
soldier made for himself is a deep and precise act of compassion.
To enliven an alchemy of such artifacts—including the bacteria
cultured from the grooves of Negro prison songs—stretches
the heart to hold an army of the lost in equal measure.

In this way, Robleto dissolves the boundaries between us
until the viewer and the participant are one. Detailing the
fragments of history, Robleto keeps the dead alive. Until we're

forced to feel the unbreakable ways we are joined, regardless of the passage of time.

This mammoth effort of detail is an instruction in presence, showing us how to embrace the scraps and fragments of life until they remind us that we are made of the same stuff. Until one day, someone with an open, precise heart will make history of us.

Robleto models the commitment to never muffle who you are and what you see, which is crucial to inhabiting your own voice. This is just as important when bringing your work into the world.

In my own journey, I've learned that I can't be all things to all people, that I can only be who I am. This has freed me immensely. For instance, I recently gave a seminar to business CEOs. My starting point was that I don't know what it takes to be a business leader or a CEO. That's not my job.

My job is to explore the inner life we all share and how we meet the world with our soul. It's their job to apply whatever speaks to them to how they live. And so, whatever your calling, I support you wholeheartedly in not trying to shape your hard-earned wisdom to fit a particular audience. I encourage you to be who you are completely, no matter who you're with. Whether you're working with bankers, engineers, or hospice nurses, they are the ones who have the expertise to make good use of whatever you share.

My experience has been that it's more important to go deep than wide. This doesn't mean that I'm not sensitive to the particular circumstances of those I meet. But under whatever histories we wear or ambitions we dream of or roles we struggle to fit, we are all naked and vulnerable.

In the same spirit, when I speak at medical schools, I'm not a doctor or a nurse, and so I can't add anything to the technical knowledge they need. But as a cancer survivor, I know a great deal about life and death and how the two are up in our face and heart constantly. This is what I can share.

So whatever your gift, I urge you to be yourself so you can open up a heart space for the people you are privileged to journey with, whether they are surviving the death of a loved one, or are social workers or grief counselors or a convention of mayors. Offer yourself out of the work you've already done in becoming who you are, and give of yourself from there.

We must try to value our deepest presence, and summon the courage to have that presence be our instrument. Later in life, the vibrant Walt Whitman said: "If I had gone directly to the people, read my poems, faced the crowds, got into immediate touch with Tom, Dick, and Harry instead of waiting to be interpreted, I'd have had my audience at once."

When starting out, the great sculptor Auguste Rodin had a penetrating and generous drawing teacher, Horace Lecoq de Boisbaudran, who taught him that "One looks with the eyes, but one sees with the heart."

Your heart is such a fine, fine brush and your feelings are its paints. Today is the only canvas.

The commitment to never muffle the full
terrain of who you are and what you see is
crucial to inhabiting your own voice.

An Invitation to Listen
to the Fragments of History

• Explore Robleto's felt use of physical fragments
  from history by gathering a few pieces from the
  history around you. They might be from your
  relational life or from the history of where you
  live. Spread these fragments before you and be
  present with them until they begin to tell their
  story. In your journal, record their story.

• In conversation with a friend or loved one, tell the story
  of the historical fragments that you have gathered and
  try to imagine the forms of life that came before you.

• Later, gather a few physical fragments from your own
  journey. As above, spread these fragments before
  you and be present with them until they begin to
  reveal your deeper story. In your journal, weave these
  fragments as symbols of your own authority of being.
  Turn to these fragment-totems when you need to.

The Energy of Hope

I believe that teaching, reading, and writing all have to do with searching. Each involves searching for Wholeness through dialogue and experience. When that search involves other living things, we find ourselves in the province of learning and teaching. When that search involves other living things that are not present or of our time, the dialogue takes the form of reading. And when that search involves things that are present and living but not yet visible or known, we have entered the creative realm, which includes writing.

These forms of search are really inseparable. They constantly impact each other. In truth, a teacher is someone who is actively involved in all three forms of search—whether they have a classroom or not, whether they are reading the wind instead of a book, or whether they ever write it down or not. At the heart of it, learning is really seeing, while writing is really internalizing what is seen through the life of our expression. And teaching is asking questions about what is seen and taken to heart—in an effort that if honestly entered usually leads to seeing further and taking in more.

One of the most shocking moments during my illness with cancer occurred when I was desperately in search of some poetry that could help me live. Almost everything I turned to was dark, chaotic, and surly, and ultimately of no use. I was bereft. It made me re-evaluate the journey of literature. For if we can't add to our authenticity of living, writing becomes just another parlor game on the edge of the abyss. This disturbed me and forced me to uplift myself while not minimizing the difficulties I faced. Since that time, I try to render both the light and the thing that blocks the light, whatever form it takes, the way an explorer tries to leave an accurate map. Now, I write in service of the light that seeps through every crack, and in the service of useful maps.

Now, I read things mostly in an effort to become whole: Abraham Heschel, Naomi Shihab Nye, Carl Jung, the Upanishads, Chuang Tzu, Ursula Le Guin, Lao Tzu, and Tu Fu. They all have something in common with an eternal principle that informs modern recovery programs. That principle says that healing takes place in the presence of another. Very often, when literature or art does not enable healing, it's because the writer or artist, the steward of the message, is not present. Most of what I read when I was ill didn't help because the writer had sealed off all possibility of communion with the reader. All hope was precluded, making the utterance useless.

It is a misnomer that hope is idealistic and saccharine. In actuality, hope is the energy of life filtering through the honesty of all its impediments. In our modern era, we endure a culture of hiddenness and denial, which has left most people frantically searching for the true energy of hope.

Hope is the energy of life filtering through the honesty of all its impediments.

An Invitation to Explore the Energy of Hope

- Read something you are drawn to. Read it several times. Identify one thing in the piece that calls you back to it. If it is a tiger that is mentioned, research tigers. If it is a part of the world you've never been to, research that part of the world. Also learn more about the life of the person who wrote this piece. Then, in your journal, explore what touches you about the piece, the part in the piece that calls to you, and the life of the person who wrote the piece.

- In conversation with a friend or loved one, discuss a time when the energy of life filtered through an obstacle you were facing.

Fitting Things Together

I am in awe of the relational power of creation. That is, what happens between the thing created and the creator. Just as the transformative moments of love lead us into a sweet place where what is loved and the lover merge, become one, and are no longer distinguishable—so too with the created piece and the thing compelling the artist to create it.

In this regard, Albert Schweitzer might be considered a more meaning-bearing artist than Andy Warhol. For Schweitzer appears to have been more deeply transformed by his journey to create a hospital in Africa than Warhol, who seemed to function as an innovative, though rarely affected, catalyst in his prodigious output of painting after avant-garde painting.

The transformative power of creativity is available to everyone, whether we have talent or not, for ability or prowess is not the point. This notion of art is focused more on the impact of the process than on the result, more in keeping with the fundamental sense that gives rise to Tibetan sand mandalas and Navajo sand paintings.

In both cases, artists devote themselves to the creation of intricate sand murals that sometimes take months to form. For Tibetan artists, the entire venture is a prayer to the impermanence of life. Once complete, they chant and bow and wipe aside the painstakingly inlaid colored sand, as if the painting never happened. Navajo artists simply walk away and let the Great Spirit finish their painting by making it disappear under the fingers of the wind. For these indigenous artists, the journey matters more than the beautiful artifacts their efforts may produce.

It's interesting to note that the word *art* comes from the Latin *ars*, which means *craft* or *skill*. But what kind of skill? If we look further, the word's Indo-European root means *to fit together*. At the heart of it, we could say that *art involves the craft or skill of fitting things together*. As such, it is a lifelong capacity that lives in everyone, for part of being human is the never-ending task of fitting things together. So, art is a creative, expressive means by which we come to understand our human experience.

The word *art* also shares a common root with such words as *arm, harmony, ordinary,* and *rite*. Such a confluence points to a perennial purpose of art: *to discover harmony through the ordinary ritual of making things.* Whether we create a wheel, a garden, or a relationship, it is by fitting things together into a working whole that we make sense of being alive. The capacity of art that lives in everyone is a seed of transformation we each carry, a way of knowing and making that can lead us to what is true over what is great, a way of searching that can lead us to what is worth celebrating over any short-lived illusion of celebrity.

By trying to create, we are created. By trying to express, we are expressed. By trying to discover meaning, we become meaningful. So, the measure of great art can be understood, not so much by the beauty achieved in birthing a singular piece, but more by the transformation it births in us for the journey of creating it. It is not the thing created that renews us, but the creative act that restores us to our place in the Mystery.

We are all artists, wanting to create and waiting to be created—each of us shaped by our devotions and trials in fitting things together. Everyone is privileged to live the artist's journey, if we only dare to voice what we feel. When we do, passages unfold.

Early on, most of us use our gifts as a way to learn about the world we've been born into. This is a time of firsts.

Everything is new and everything triggers wonder. Once the world becomes somewhat known, the hunger for wonder continues, and we begin to seek out what is unique, what is special. Often, this is part of our search for identity, to find one's place as distinguished from everyone and everything else.

In time though, through some clear or ambiguous suffering, most of us, if resilient enough to keep growing, find ourselves transformed and humbled into an eternal perspective that makes us look for comfort and meaning in what we have in common with the living. Now we search for the Living Center and Source that lies at the heart of everything. A different kind of identity is found there that is more empowering and enduring.

For those who continue to be shaped by their journey, life becomes a sacred expedition of seeking moments of love, epiphany, and wisdom. Then, the art we leave behind is the trail of a timeless want to bear witness and belong to something larger than one's self. Over a lifetime, we experience an evolving sense of fitting things together through which we are put together.

Of course, the journey is fraught with obstacles and derailments, all of which contribute to shaping us further. Ironically, we all begin wanting to be instrumental, wanting to alter the world and achieve great things. Yet, if blessed, we are honed and pared down to a hollow bone that longs to be an instrument, through which the greater forces play their music.

At each juncture, we can stray from our capacity to fit things together. When we lose access to our creativity, we lose access to wonder. This in turn distances us from the resource that is life. We may continue to gather and sort enormous amounts of information, but this is not the same as releasing life-force by fitting things together. Rather, gathering and sorting is like hoarding mounds of kindling with no way to light it. A poignant example of this can be found in one of the last letters Charles Darwin ever wrote:

> Up to the age of thirty, or beyond it, poetry of many kinds, such as the works of Milton, Gray, Byron, Wordsworth, Coleridge, and Shelley, gave me great pleasure. . . . But now for many years I cannot endure to read a line of poetry. . . . My mind seems to have become a kind of machine for grinding general laws out of large collections of facts . . . and if I had to live my life again, I would have made a rule to read some poetry and listen to some music at least once every week. . . . The loss of these tastes is a loss of happiness and may possibly be injurious to the intellect, and more probably to the moral character, by enfeebling the emotional part of our nature.

The journey of art and its impact on each of us is a powerful source of wakefulness. Yet the power of art to shape us has been muffled in our society until art has been quarantined as an abstract pursuit of beauty or a sophisticated form of entertainment. Nothing could be further from the truth. Meaningful art, enduring art—and the transformative process it reveals—keeps us alive.

So where are you in the lifelong quest to fit things together? What are you creating and how is it creating you? What have you tried to do and how has it undone your early intent? How is life making you whole? Just what is the mirror of the world holding up to you? And what is it trying to say?

The capacity of art that lives in everyone is a seed of transformation we each carry, a way of knowing and making that can lead us to what is true over what is great.

An Invitation to Relate to the Creative Process

- In your journal, describe the relationship between you and something you created: how it drew you to its possibility, how its process of being birthed led you, and how you were changed by the experience of creating it.

- In conversation with a friend or loved one, tell the story of someone you admire who taught you about the craft or skill of fitting things together.

Part 2

Being Shaped by Life

As the sea carves the mouth of every shore, as the wind bends the top of every tree, as fire makes the most stubborn of creatures let go, the forces of life carve and mold us. Every day, our will meets all that is larger than us, and that meeting wears us into a receptacle of acceptance and surrender, in which our care and expression is all that's left.

This process is often hard and unrelenting. Yet, in time, we are worn open like bones hollowed into flutes. And it's the life of expression moving through us that releases a music that is at once timeless and extremely personal. The songs that play through us are the basic human truths that help us live. This part of the book explores how the forces of life refine how we take in life and how we turn that life-force into acts of care and expression.

By diving down and coming up, we discover our voice. By drifting in the immensity, we discover the power of art. By living a making, we can unravel the riddle of a self, which is necessary because our self is the only window we have into existence.

Ultimately, we are here to bear witness to the miracles and hardships of life, through the instrument that we each become. It is the livelihood that comes from bearing witness and creating that pays us with ever more life.

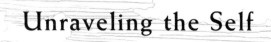

Unraveling the Self

If I am not for myself, who will be?
If I am only for myself, what am I?
If not now, when?
RABBI HILLEL

The Riddle of a Self

The quote cited by Rabbi Hillel that begins this section is perhaps the greatest haiku ever expressed. It was written in the first century BC, hundreds of years before the form of haiku was conceived. It captures the riddle of a self, which we all have to enter: how to be who we are everywhere and how not to be confined to only who we are.

One the one hand, we have to solidify a self from which to navigate our way through life. On the other hand, we need to fill that self with everything we are not, so we can keep growing and joining with other life while we are here. The self is a container for the portion of Spirit we each are born to steward while alive. As such, our container needs to be sturdy and hollow, so that Spirit and life can move through us. If we thicken our container too much, we risk not being hollow enough for life to move through us. Then we live behind a thickened wall of self. The life of expression helps keep the container of a self hollow.

In support of being who we are, E. E. Cummings offered this to a graduating high school class in 1955:

> To be nobody—but—yourself—in a world which is doing its best, night and day, to make you everybody else—means to fight the hardest battle which any human being can fight; and never stop fighting.

In support of opening ourselves to others, Plato said that we are born whole but we need each other to be complete. In truth, we need each other to inhabit life fully. The wonderful poet Denise Levertov makes this freshly clear in her poem "The Secret."

There, she recounts how two young girls rush to her, giddy to say that they have discovered the secret of life in a line of one of her poems. Ecstatic, they thank her and run off. But Levertov yearns to know which line in which poem! We know very little without each other. Alone without the secret, Levertov blesses the two girls for their discovery and for believing that there is a secret in the first place.

Essentially, we become as we go, unraveling the layers of our self, one mask at a time, till nothing else can be removed. Then we are who we are everywhere. Along the way, writing authentically has led me to learn about others while exploring myself and to learn about myself while exploring others.

In retrieving my epic poem, *Fire Without Witness*, I had to tell the stories of dozens of characters, biblical and mythic. In doing so, I had to pour my own humanity into several different containers and move around in their skin, in their lives, in their conflicts and hidden loves. Through the journey of becoming other voices, I clarified my own.

As I shared earlier, I fell into my cancer journey shortly after finishing *Fire Without Witness*. Then I was forced to be thoroughly and only myself. Then I had to face the prospect of living and dying firsthand. For through the journey of facing the one life I've been given, I discovered my kinship to all living things. This led to my autobiographical book *Inside the Miracle*. Over time, I learned that when we write about ourselves deeply enough, we discover the world. And when we write about others deeply enough, we discover ourselves.

It doesn't matter whether we enter our explorations through the stories of others or through the story of our own life. Either way, we can arrive at truth and meaning. I have found over the years that I am in a long recurring cycle of cleaning the lens of my self by writing autobiographically, so I can become others and tell their stories through fiction, history, and memoir. Then the stories of others grow who I am until I need to self-express to clean my lens again, so I can continue to take in and tell the stories of others. And on it goes.

Regardless of the art form that calls us, we must find the vibrant center of truth that waits beneath all names, whether by going into ourselves completely or out of ourselves completely. In this way, the life of expression is always concerned with the internal search for meaning. In this way, we are constantly writing our way into our lives and living our way into our writing. In this way, autobiography becomes a conversation between our soul and the Oversoul. Whether swimming with or against the current, a fish can never be understood outside of the water it lives in. And an individual soul can never be understood apart from the world it is born into.

Before my cancer journey, I was a driven artist. But on the other side, landing in ordinary life, I had lost my creative drive. This frightened me. It took several months for me to realize that instead of being driven, I was drawn to things. The way a river rushes mightily and noisily to join the sea, my drive had given way to deeper waters. And there, I found more freedom and joy.

Now, I can only say that a poet's job is to follow everything that is life-giving until we embody and evoke the deeper truth that holds life up. The surest way to do this is to inhabit the riddle of a self. As the poet, essayist, and playwright Elizabeth Alexander says, "You have to tell your own story simultaneously as you hear and tell the stories of others."

The life of expression helps keep the container of a self hollow.

An Invitation to Connect
Your Story to Others

* In your journal, describe a time when the container
  of your self was too thick or too thin. Turn this
  exploration into an autobiographical writing. After
  surfacing this personal story, explore how what
  you have experienced relates to what others have
  experienced. Try to name this common journey.

* In conversation with a friend or loved one, describe
  a time when you observed someone being wrongly
  blamed for a turn of events. Evolve this sharing
  into a story that you write by pouring yourself into
  this person's shoes. After surfacing this fictional
  story, explore how you relate to the character's
  experience. Try to name this common journey.

Love at First Sight

To be a poet is to be healthfully possessed with the instinct to stay authentic. In this regard, William Butler Yeats says:

> Genius is a crisis that joins the buried self,
> for certain moments, to our daily mind.

Much of our daily life is spent making it through that crisis. The difference between the authentic life and the hidden life is that the poet in us seeks opportunities to *break through*, while our hidden self distorts the task and seeks only opportunities to *break from*.

I mentioned earlier that the crisis that started me writing was a broken heart, my first deep opportunity to break from or break through. My Dulcinea had auburn hair and lips that knew nothing but the secret of their softness. I was ruined before the glow even thinned. She, of course, left to live her life, and I began to break. In my heartache, I began to utter to myself, to speak freely at the air, and once I healed, I never stopped.

It is important to affirm that this dynamic of releasing our particular genius through the living of our ordinary lives speaks to the poetry of authenticity—not just writing, but of an aliveness that is dormant and waiting to wake in everyone. If surfacing our buried self is what we're after, loving is how we get there.

So let's consider love at first sight. While this can certainly happen, it is love at first true seeing that brings us alive, despite the numbness and woundedness that tripping about the world can bring. I can see you every day for years, saying hello at the office. We find each other pleasant and cordial.

But this one day, when I am heartsick because my father is dying, and you are too exhausted to keep your mask in place, we see each other deeply and freshly for the first time. And I'm stunned; I never realized it was you. Now, after all these years, we truly meet and love each other completely at first true seeing.

This is how we rediscover the world and the Mystery that informs the world, one true seeing at a time, as the clouds that hover around our head and heart are blown aside unexpectedly.

Yet how do we take in what comes from these fresh, unpacked moments in which meaning presents itself? We do this by committing to the effort to listen, reflect, and express, which are the basic, authentic steps of true perception.

It helps to remember that whatever the process, it can be broken down into basic steps. When a center fielder is in a slump, his batting coach takes him aside and has him return to the basics of his swing. When in sync, the back swing, swing, and follow-through are all one motion. But when faltering, the center fielder must concentrate on each component separately in order to return to his form. Because sometimes we rush our swing and don't follow through or hang too long in our back swing.

Likewise, when at our best, we take in the world in one sweet motion: listening, reflecting, and expressing in a seamless effort. But when we falter, we need to slow down and recover the individual steps. When we listen, we simply take in things as they are without processing them. When we reflect, we hold what we have seen or heard and circle it, trying to discern what it means. And when we express, we ask ourselves, "How do I feel about what I've seen or heard?"

Often, in our fear and pain, we rush these steps into one hurried reach, making conclusions before we've had a chance to take things in and reflect. The natural sequence of listening, reflecting, and expressing is tantamount to breathing. When we breathe, we inhale till we reach that still point at the top of our inhalation, where we briefly hold and then exhale. Normally, this is all one motion, but meditation helps us break down our breathing into its basic rhythms. In perceiving, we inhale by listening, reflect at our still point, and then exhale by expressing what we're feeling back into the world.

To slow down and reclaim the very steps of perception lets us inhabit our authenticity, which lets us keep falling in love with everything and everyone we meet. This renders us vulnerable, malleable, forgeable. Like someone who gasps awake after a deep sleep, we break through and wake, a day at a time, in order to release our gifts into the world.

It is love at first true seeing that brings us alive, despite the numbness and woundedness that tripping about the world can bring.

An Invitation to Listen, Reflect, and Express

- Take a walk and practice listening, reflecting, and expressing as you encounter the world around you. Later, in your journal, write about the series of perceptions you have taken in by describing what you've seen and heard, then reflecting on what it all means, and then by expressing what you feel about what you've taken in and what you think it means.

- In conversation with a friend or loved one, tell the story of a moment of love at first true seeing that you've experienced. Describe the difference between how you experienced the person before and after this awakening. Later, write a reflection or a story about the impact of love at first true seeing.

Living a Making

The professional photographer takes assignments from "without"
. . . the creative photographer takes assignments from "within."
The conflict from assignments—from "without" versus those
from "within"—often perplexes the serious photographer.
ANSEL ADAMS

When finding my way, I came home from college to have a classic argument with my father. Over dinner the first night, I declared to him with excitement that I was a poet. I hadn't yet written anything but knew it was true. He was incredulous and frustrated and loudly asked, "How are you going to make a living?" I'm not sure where it came from in me, but I looked at him and said, "I'm going to live a making." I confess that I've spent much of my life learning what that means. And it is living a making for so many years that has led me to the place of true meeting that waits under all our struggles.

I have learned that making a living is tending the assignments that come from "without," while living a making is tending the assignments that come from "within." Making a living is how we survive, but living a making is how we thrive. We need the strength and resilience to do both.

There is always a tension between surviving and thriving, between the assignments that come from "without" and the assignments that come from "within," and between making a living and living a making. Part of the journey of individuation is withstanding the tension of both until they work hand in hand.

Recently, I received a heartfelt email from my godson, Eli (my dear friend Robert's son). As a young artist finding his way, he asked me the very questions I asked when I was his age. Though I have no answers, I was touched that he asked. I emailed him back, sharing my wonderings along the way about the tensions of being an artist in the world:

Dear Eli,

Your questions about living a creative life raise issues I've wrestled with my entire life. To begin with, I have always known from the time I was your age that a creative force lived in me, fueled me, and shaped me. I knew that in order for me to be who I was put here to be, I needed to stay committed and devoted to that call. And so, I have always respected the challenge of being a parent, vowing to only bring a child into this world if I could be completely committed to that child's life. I feared I would either be a bad parent, unable to veer from my creative force enough to be there for that child, or that my love of such a child would keep me from living out my creative call. Ultimately, out of respect for what is required, I have always been clear that I didn't want to have children. Some along the way have thought me selfish for being so devoted, but this creative force is how I breathe. If I don't honor it, a part of me will die. Only you can know how essential this creative force is in you.

On the other beautiful side of this is your dear father, my oldest friend—really my brother. He and your mother have brought you and your dear brother and sister into the world so lovingly, so devotedly. We wouldn't be having this conversation without the commitment of their love. And I am so grateful the three of you are here. I held you the day you were born and sensed what a gentle soul you are—even then. And throughout your life, your father has remained devoted to his art.

This raises something that I have only learned after many years of wrestling with the creative force, no matter how it shows itself. That is, we are most alive and happiest while loving and creating, continually shaped by our total involvement. I started out deeply committed, hoping to write maybe one or two great poems along the way. Yet, when I had cancer in my thirties—and your father helped save my life, and I his, from alcoholism—I began to discover that living is the original art.

I can only conclude that living wholeheartedly while holding nothing back will bring you into a beautifully charged relationship with living your art and the art of living.

Two more parenting examples are Picasso and the great poet William Carlos Williams. While Picasso couldn't help but follow his enormous gift, he littered Europe with children conceived by many different partners, children he seldom had contact with. This has always served as a specter of the kind of parent I never wanted to be. On the other side of the spectrum, the amazing William Carlos Williams became a pediatrician so he could make a living without having to depend on his poetry to make money. He also became a doctor so he could stay close to the pulse of life and death, which he knew would inform his poetry. In time, he had three children: two sons and a daughter.

Honestly, it can be done either way. There is no wrong path. The most important thing is to know yourself, your creative force, and your own nature, as intimately as possible, so you can make the choices that are most integral with your own true nature.

I also want to speak of my lifelong struggle to be in a balanced and healthy relationship with my creative force. You are young and, I believe, exactly where you need to be, exploring your devotion to what brings you alive, to see where that takes you, to see how it shapes you. In time, you will see if those who love you can recognize and support that this creative force is part of who you are. In time, you will see if they can welcome your creativity into whatever life you might build together.

When your age, I was a driven artist, almost to a fault. For the creative force, if allowed, will use us up, as it did Van Gogh. I've discovered, after soaring and sputtering, again and again, that the only way to be in healthy relationship with our creative force is to integrate it with our life in the world.

When your father and I were a few years on the other side of my cancer and his active drinking, we were eating lunch one sober, summer day in downtown Albany, both of us with hands numb from neuropathy. Me from the chemo I endured and your father from the advanced stages of alcoholism he suffered. It was a beautiful day and we ate our sandwiches in the sun. Out of our silence, your dad said to me, "I'm an alcoholic, but you're a make-oholic." I was stunned at the truth of this. For anything, even our creativity, can become an addiction. Ever since, I have been aware and respectful of the need to have balance and the love of others in my life.

It's humbling and inspiring that, no matter how many years I've been devoted to the craft of perception, I still wake every day with a sense of starting over and a yearning to get as close to the pulse of life as possible. And I admit that, whether aware of it or not, I write about what I need to draw my soul into the world. So, my books are my teachers. Once I understood this, I found more joy in writing. Now I welcome this vast unknowing. Each book leads to the next. Questions unravel into deeper questions. And here I am: following one question to the next, book by book.

The truth is that I barely understand half of what comes through me. The other half leads me. Still, I know if I give myself over to the creative force, it will use me up. It's my heart that keeps me here in the world, and the creative force rushing through my heart is what makes any of what you might read.

All this to say—only you have the wisdom, waiting like a seed inside your heart, and your conversation with life will reveal that personal wisdom to you, in time. The only oracle to consult is what feels ultimately true for you in any given moment.

All this to say—the more you trust your heart and stay in conversation with life, the more deeply life will speak to you, as you live. And when you feel overwhelmed, remember that your heart is stronger and larger than any one feeling it may experience.

Honestly, I am just sharing where life has taken me, and my path may not be yours. But I can affirm that you are not crazy and that as a creative soul, you're in a noble lineage. It is fine to be driven, and fine to be drawn, and fine to struggle with these things. What else would we do?

Please know that I feel blessed to have you in my life.

My love,
Mark

*Making a living is how we survive, but
living a making is how we thrive. We need
the strength and resilience to do both.*

An Invitation to Name
Your True Nature

- The Abenaki elder Joseph Bruchac says, "A friend is
  a person you tell your true name." If you were to
  name your true self—in the spirit of how Native
  Americans name themselves by phrases glimpsed
  from the natural world—what phrase or two
  would you start with? Explore this in your journal
  and tell one part of your story by which you have
  come to befriend and know your true self.

- In conversation with a friend or loved one, describe
  an experience in which you found yourself living
  a making, where your engagement in a detailed
  process of creating, building, or repairing brought
  you more alive. How did your immersion in the
  process affect your outlook and behavior?

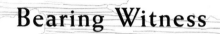

Bearing Witness

*The work of the poet
is to name what is holy,
a task fit for Eternity,
or the small Eden of this hour.*

DIANE ACKERMAN

Looking at Life Together

Not everything that is faced can be changed,
but nothing can be changed until it is faced.
JAMES BALDWIN

Bearing witness is one of the primary ways that human beings hold each other up and help each other grow. Bearing witness is also one of the primary functions of art.

Social media is becoming a modern form of bearing witness that is adding to our communal sense of art. In 2010, it was the viral use of Facebook that helped ignite the Arab Spring, a revolutionary wave of democratic protests and demonstrations that led to civil wars in oppressive societies in North Africa and the Middle East. Here in America, the ability of citizens to film events in real time has led to an irrefutable bearing witness of excessive force by police.

This all speaks to the timeless power of naming things for what they are in the open. Earlier, I mentioned the luminous poet Czeslaw Milosz. In 1981, Milosz was invited to give a series of talks at Harvard as part of the ongoing Charles Eliot Norton Lectures. The talks were published a few years later as his remarkable book *The Witness of Poetry*. In these deep and sweeping talks, Milosz articulates his belief that poetry should be "a passionate pursuit of the real." He challenges us to reclaim the power of art to mirror both the failings and blessings of the world. He offers that art, in particular poetry, is our enduring crucible in which to face the moral challenges of our time.

I would add that the chief function of art in all its forms is to marry what *is* with what *can be*. By voicing the truth of things as they are while enlivening our better angels, art helps us live. Gandhi valued poetry as an inner companion on his lifelong journey of activism. When journalists criticized his friend, the poet Rabindranath Tagore, as hiding in poetry from the challenges that India faced, Gandhi replied: "I regard the Poet as a sentinel warning us against the approaching enemies called Bigotry, Lethargy, Intolerance, Ignorance, [and] Inertia."

Not only do artists and poets mirror our best and worst aspects, but they are often diagnosticians of the social body. The legendary blues musician Mose Allison tells the story of a prominent white educator who was studying the culture of the Hopi, the desert-dwelling Native American tribe of the Southwest. He found it strange that almost all Hopi music was about water and asked one of the native musicians why. The old Hopi man put down his wooden flute and explained that so much of their music was about water because that was what they had the least of. And then he told the white man, "Most of your music is about love." This is another form of bearing witness, to uncover and mirror the weakening patterns of our society.

Yet a poet also stands as a sentinel on the edge of the Mystery, working as an inner explorer, trying to integrate the lessons of both the inner and the outer world.

We also bear witness when looking at life together. I have a friend who wrote me about the meaning of a poem I sent her. It really doesn't matter which poem or what it said. The reason I mention it is because, as the "author," I don't have any advantage in uncovering its meaning. I just write them, that is retrieve them, trying to stay out of the way, trying not to corrupt what comes through with too many of my own preferences for meaning. The fact is that my interpretation is no more clear or relevant than anyone else's. My friend's guess is as good as mine. It is really the conversations that arise from circling what is retrieved that evoke the real poetry. In this, we are all poet-fishermen, netting experience as we go and dumping what we catch and drag on board, to look at it together.

It makes me think of Jackson Pollock's method of painting, how he would let the brush hover over the canvas, not directly touching it but letting the paint have the space to free-fall and find its deeper flow. He wasn't just throwing paint, but giving up his predeterminations of where the paint belonged. Instead, he entered a relationship with the unseeable space in between through which deeper patterns landed on the canvas.

It is this interplay with the space in between that Martin Buber speaks of as the place of true speech, the enlivening of I-Thou, where the unrehearsed dialogue with God arises between two living centers. Letting go of our predeterminations and listening to the space in between is what allows the meaning of life to find its deeper expression through us. The poetry exists in that space in between: between the poet and the Source, between life and our experience, and between the two or more who try to make sense of it.

Every time we venture out into the world, we are both looking at life and bearing witness. It is how we keep current, how we keep the soul close to the surface without uprooting it from its home deep within us.

I was recently sitting on a sunny afternoon in Washington Square Park in New York City, when I realized that as much as I've learned from nature, I've learned even more from the human forest. I love the unrehearsed interplay of human beings crisscrossing as we reach for light and love, bearing witness to each other. This one day there was a magician weaving his magic, while couples were lounging in the grass. And someone in the shade was hanging their head, while old men in the sun were playing chess. And at the head of a path, a trio of young musicians were lost in their jam, while a young man was bursting about with a sign that read, "Free Hugs."

We are here for such a short time, and the truth of our experience holds far greater stories than the grandest fiction.

The chief function of art in all its forms is to marry what is with *what can be. By voicing the truth of things as they are while enlivening our better angels, art helps us live.*

An Invitation to Bear Witness

- In your journal, write a poem or tell a story that marries what *is* with what *can be.*

- In conversation with a friend or loved one, look at some aspect of life together—something like truth, faith, doubt, or fear. Describe your latest encounter with this aspect of life and bear witness to each other's journey.

- Later, in your journal, examine in detail both the harshness and beauty braided around you in the world, and bear witness to the whole truth of what you see.

The Power of Art

*Here is a great truth, which is valid at every stage of the
quest. If we refuse, or are not able to express, to make
actual in some form or other our vision, such as it is at
any point, then we are not only unable to go forward to
the next step but we are probably in for a regression.*

*For instance, a dream or vision will retreat again
into the unconscious and have no substance unless
written or perhaps painted—made visible, audible, or
tangible in some way—[then] shared with one other
and attended to so that it alters our attitude.*

HELEN LUKE

One of the first readings I gave in New York City was at a bar in Greenwich Village. A crowd was assembling when a young man came in distraught and said, "I just saw a mugging on the way over here. I was so upset I stopped to write a poem." Somebody else bellowed from across the room, "Sure beats stopping the mugging."

This story illustrates how our modern sensibility has evolved to where we use our skills to separate ourselves from the life going on around us, to comment on it, while staying removed and protected. In this way, the words, the paint, even the music becomes a clear wall behind which we can see what's going on yet not be touched. But the courage to truly bear witness joins living things and empowers us to act on each other's behalf. This is the kind of bearing witness that yields art, that makes the artist whole, that offers healing to other living things.

A touching example of bearing witness is the story in Pablo Neruda's memoirs when he goes to visit a mining site in Antofagasta, Chile. There, a man comes up from the bowels of the earth, his face completely caked. The miner reaches for Neruda and calls him "my brother" because his poems had affirmed the miner's life for years. This meant more to Neruda than the numerous awards and global renown he'd achieved.

History is a cycle in which we are reduced again and again by suffering and conflict to the beauty and miracle of just being alive. The power of art enlivens this transformation. Gandhi said, "The poet will sing the true note after the war is over." But there can be no art or poetry without expression and reciprocity to ignite true presence in the world.

In 1978, NBC broadcast *Holocaust*, a television miniseries in four parts. Directed by Marvin J. Chomsky, who also directed ABC's unprecedented miniseries *Roots*, *Holocaust* unfolds the story of a fictional family of German Jews as they are torn apart and dispersed throughout Europe and thrown into the camps. Though criticized by some, including Holocaust survivor and Nobel Prize winner Elie Wiesel, who described it as "untrue and offensive," this flawed attempt to bear witness to this incomprehensible genocide stirred the conscience of the first post–World War II generation in America and Europe.

When shown in West Germany, the miniseries caused the next generation to explore their pain in remembering the Holocaust, which led them to question their parents and elders: How did this happen? How could it have happened here? Did you know about it? Did you have anything to do with it? The response to the broadcast was so strong in postwar West Germany that the parliament extended the statute of limitations on Nazi war crimes.

This is a dramatic example of how the power of art can reawaken our always-needed conversation about what it means to be human and to live together. That the miniseries was flawed only confirms that bearing witness can be done whether the art that stirs us is a masterpiece or not. It's more important to shout "fire" in a theater or "murder" in the square than to sing it on pitch.

In the wake of World War II, Abstract Expressionism (1949–1960) was a global exploration by artists attempting to make sense of the devastation, indignity, and ruin of a broken world. Things could no longer go on as they were: not as nations, not in education, not in our way of seeing or expressing who we were or what we'd been through.

The very means and manner of art began to break down and reform, taking another leap away from a straightforward, literal representation of life into the whirl and energetic chaos of what on the surface seemed abstract, but which was creating portals for reflection on the realities of the dismantled world around us. In 1952, Jean Dubuffet (1901–1985) emerged as a leader in the European arm of this movement, which he termed Art Brut (Raw Art). In the same year, the French writer Michel Tapié published a book referring to Abstract Expressionism as *Un Art Autre* (Art of Another Kind).

As with all innovation, the curators of the day were slow to receive what was new. A few years earlier, in 1950 in New York City, a movement arose when in April of that year, at Studio 35, a group of eighteen painters (including Jackson Pollock, Willem de Kooning, Barnett Newman, and Mark Rothko) and ten sculptors joined together to protest a juried exhibition at the Metropolitan Museum of Art, claiming the Museum was antagonistic to "advanced art." As a result, the New York Abstract Expressionists were labeled the "Irascibles." At the same time, Montreal's avant-garde movement, the Automatistes, boycotted a conservatively juried show at the Montreal Museum of Fine Arts, for which they were labeled the "Rebels."

Though the efforts of the Irascibles and the Rebels didn't change the stance of the museums, their steadfastness solidified a worldwide movement in abstract art that is now, almost seventy years later, foundational to our time and the centerpiece of these museums. Again, we're shown that staying true to who we are and gathering our presence authentically is a compelling and nonviolent means of social change.

In indigenous cultures, poets have always been the ones to carry the tribe's history—its joys and traumas. That sacred role has been resisted and muffled in modern times. The performance artist Marina Abramović has assumed that role for her native Yugoslavia for much of her life.

Abramović was born in Belgrade in what was Yugoslavia in 1946, the daughter of strict, military heroes who had prominent positions in Tito's postwar government. "When people ask me where I am from," she says, "I never say Serbia. I always say I come from a country that no longer exists." As happens throughout history, a war-torn land produces a global, timeless citizen whose voice belongs to no one but speaks for everyone.

In 1997, she bore witness to the suffering of her native country by performing *Balkan Baroque* in the Venice Biennale. This piece involved her scrubbing clean 1,500 cow bones six hours a day for four days and weeping as she sang songs and told stories from her native country.

The power of art remains dormant until what we experience is, as Helen Luke says, "made visible, audible, or tangible in some way—[then] shared with one other and attended to so that it alters our attitude."

The first step in releasing the power of art is to see things as they are and then to dare to give voice to what we see, expressing what life is doing to us and through us. Paradoxically, giving voice to the truth of any situation liberates us, even when we feel powerless.

The dissident Russian writer, Aleksandr Solzhenitsyn (1918–2008), spent his life fighting for human rights. Among his many books, he wrote *Prussian Nights*, a book-length poem based on his experiences as a captain of an artillery battery on the Belorussian Front, which invaded East Prussia at the end of World War II.

This is the story of how he wrote that book. In July 1945, Solzhenitsyn was sentenced to an eight-year term in a forced labor camp to silence his voice. During his imprisonment, Solzhenitsyn composed all twelve thousand lines of the poem, writing a few lines each day on a bar of soap and memorizing them as his daily shower washed the lines away.

Later, he wrote how expressing this poem and composing it, line by line, helped him survive his imprisonment:

> I needed a clear head, because for two years I
> [was] writing a poem—a most rewarding poem
> that helped me not to notice what was being
> done to my body. Sometimes, while standing in a
> column of dejected prisoners, amidst the shouts
> of guards with machine guns, I felt such a rush of
> rhymes and images that I seemed to be [drifting]
> overhead. . . . At such moments, I was both free
> and happy. . . . Some prisoners tried to escape
> by smashing a car through the barbed wire. For
> me, there was no barbed wire. The head count of
> prisoners remained unchanged, but I was actually
> away on a distant flight.

Once free, he slowly penned the poem that he had memorized while in prison. In 1969, he made a recording of *Prussian Nights*. His integrity and work became known worldwide, and he was awarded the Nobel Prize for Literature in 1970 "for the ethical force with which he has pursued the indispensable traditions of Russian literature." Finally, *Prussian Nights* was published in a Russian edition in Paris in 1974, after he was expelled from his beloved Russia.

This is yet another compelling example of how giving voice to the truth is an inner form of breathing, which, like focused meditation, can help us endure the harshest circumstances.

In her essay "Poetry and Commitment," Adrienne Rich tells this more recent story:

> On July 17, 2005, the *San Francisco Chronicle* ran this headline: "Writing Poetry Was the Balm that Kept Guantanamo Prisoner from Going Mad." The story recounted how Abdul Rahim Muslim Dost, who was arrested in Afghanistan and held without charges in Guantanamo, wrote thousands of lines of poetry during his detention, scratching [line after line] with his fingernail into Styrofoam cups.

When we rely on the integrity of our heart to carry us, our ability to endure is strengthened, regardless of what is created. The act of expressing is a release of life-force that keeps creating us.

Giving voice to the truth of any situation
liberates us, even when we feel powerless.

An Invitation to Explore
the Power of Art

- Go to a museum and wander until you find a piece
  of art that touches you. Stand before it until it
  speaks to you. Imagine the person who created
  it, what it meant to them, and how it came to
  them. In your journal, explore the power of this
  piece of art and describe how it touches you.

- In your journal, write a poem or tell a story
  that mirrors the chaos or harmony of the
  world as you are experiencing it.

- In conversation with a friend or loved one, describe
  someone you admire who is a good witness in
  the world. What strength do they have that you
  can learn from? Name one step you can take
  to inhabit this strength in your own life.

Drifting in the Immensity

As the sky is reflected in water, the world is reflected in the immensity we call the inner world. We are citizens of both, seekers of both, looking for peace in both. While we take aim at goals and destinations in the outer world, a deeper part of us is adrift in the immensity of life like a fish hypnotized by the current that carries it. When carried in the inner world, we bear witness to light and depth and the impenetrable Oneness of Things.

I had a mentor, teacher, and friend who was a great witness of the light and a great student of the unseeable immensity. He was Joel Elkes, a watercolorist and doctor, a remarkable human being who died in 2015 at the age of 102. After being educated in Lithuania and Switzerland, Joel was sent by his parents to London to study medicine while they endured the Holocaust. In England, he embarked on a career that would establish him as one of the founding fathers of psychopharmacology. During this time, he began to inquire into the Divine Universals that inform life. This led him to the practice of art, where he followed the reflection of the world into the realm of the soul. The trail of that inquiry is in his paintings.

If we live long enough, life erodes us to a perfect opening. This describes Joel Elkes in all that he did. Through his opened heart came immense love. Through his opened mind came immense understanding. And through his opened eyes came his immense paintings, which belong in the lineage of those compelled by light.

In this tribe of seers, the subject—whether a water lily, a field of barley, or a sunflower—becomes an occasion by which all of life makes itself known briefly. For Joel, the subject was often bark or stone or water or patches of sky—all occasions to witness and feel the irrepressible play of light. When asked about his paintings, he said, "These paintings are all statements of the wordless within. For light is stronger than rock."

One of Joel's earlier paintings is called *Big Sky, Little Boat*. And for a man whose vision and heart ran deeper than words, this small canvas says a great deal. For each life is such a little boat drifting in the immensity, each heart and eye listening for how the sky and ocean speak to each other.

Over the years, I've learned that the closer I am to that depth, the less I have to fuss with the words. When I can be authentic, I'm much closer to the Source of All Being. The farther I stray from that center, the less accurate I am in what I say and the more complicated my language becomes. When it all seems refracted and unclear, it's a sign that I have go back to the original vision and try again, more directly in a more heartfelt way. This is the true meaning of *re-vision*, not the economic pruning of language.

Being with Joel, listening to Joel, and loving Joel deepened my understanding of what it means to be a poet. Working with Joel led me to this poem:

To Be a Poet

We are nothing but shores
laying ourselves before the
clear depth of all that is,
letting it wash over us.

In this, we are forever
translators, not through

our minds or by how we
conjugate verbs, but by
living openly on the edge.

If you want to be a poet
you must first want to be.

If you want to see God
you must first want to see.

If you want to be of use
in the endless dance
of growing into dying
and dying into growing,

become a shore and,
against all likelihood,
your voice will rise like
gulls that ride the waves.

And what is compassion but drifting in the immensity of life
with an open heart? We bump into and pass by so many torn
and budding lives along the way. Some are like us, many are not.
But under it all, we steward the same ounce of spirit carried in
skin and bone. One of our jobs, then, is to learn how to relate to
the cascade of others who rise and fall around us. The practice
of compassion is how we learn that we are each other. And the
practice of expression is how the heart knows itself.

I was recently at the Museum of Modern Art in New York City
thinking of all this, when I sat before Van Gogh's *Wheatfield with
Cypresses*, painted in 1889. I first saw this with my dear friend
Robert in 1994 when we were both newly awakened, me on the

other side of cancer and Robert on the other side of alcoholism. It still moves me. What Van Gogh did in this canvas was to render the elements beneath their solidity, revealing the space where everything is fluid—where air, fire, earth, and water are interchangeable.

Like a quantum physicist, this driven artist conjured the elemental place where everything touches everything else. It is the place Robert and I were reduced to in our suffering, the place where beauty lives under all its disguises.

And twenty-five years later, I returned to find that this ever-changing canvas—where the sky rises like the sea and the earth is on fire—this bare, essential landscape is still a mirror of the life-force that fills us.

As I sat there, this painting I so love seemed an x-ray of our human soul. The others wandering in the museum knew this to be true. I could tell by how they stopped when they came upon it. No one said a word, but I could hear the wave of fire washing in their sky. All of us bits of life-force erupting in place. I could have put a frame around the nearest stranger and hung them on the wall, and they would have been a testament to all we go through and never share.

Artists like Joel and Van Gogh are bearing witness in a fundamental way. Like a keen biologist, the deeper artist within us bears witness, not to the events that trail behind us, but to what lives beneath the skin.

The practice of compassion is how we learn that we are each other. And the practice of expression is how the heart knows itself.

An Invitation to Understand Your Care

- In your journal, describe an early experience
  of compassion, when you opened your heart to
  someone because of a joy or pain that you had in
  common. How did this experience of compassion
  change you? How did it change the relationship?

- In conversation with a friend or loved one,
  describe a time when you felt compassion for
  someone, though you had no way to relate to
  their experience. What enabled you to stretch
  your care this far? How did this experience change
  you? How did it change the relationship?

Listening

Aloneness is indivisible and loneliness is separation.
. . . Aloneness is the purgation of all motives, of all
pursuits of desire, of all ends. . . . It is the aloneness
of being; it is uncorrupted, rich, complete.
KRISHNAMURTI

In many ways, writing is listening and simply taking notes. One of the reasons I love the process of writing is that it enables me to listen until my loneliness opens into a blessed sense of aloneness. The gift of deep silence is that it allows us to let go of what we want so we can receive what we have.

I've always been a learner of the heart, not a specialist of the mind. I can dissect and hone and prune away the excess. But the shimmer of Wholeness and the dynamics of Oneness show themselves when we can absorb and integrate rather than sort and choose.

As a young writer, I would try so hard to be a mirror, to reflect back to everything its color and verve. But as a more experienced writer, I try to be a window now, to open a threshold between people and the inner world.

Being still and listening allows us to behold what is before us. The deepest form of bearing witness is to behold another in all their innocence. This is the key to love. To listen until the noise of the world subsides. To listen until the noise of the mind subsides. To listen until the noise of our wounds subsides. To listen until we only hear the life before us.

Here's a story about listening. Legend has it that Christopher Dock, a Mennonite schoolmaster in Colonial

Pennsylvania, would come to his classroom early and, with no one there, he would kneel behind his lectern and recite each of his students' names under his breath, holding them in his heart. In this way, he would pray for them. He did this daily. And one day, after a lifetime of teaching, he shuffled in early and beheld each of his students, one by one, each in his heart. Midway, he died on his knees behind his lectern as the sheet filled with names dropped from his hand like a leaf.

Now the question arises, which served his students more? His beholding them with compassion each day before they arrived? Or his critical honing of their minds? And which serves us more: beholding the world with compassion as we meet it, or chopping a path through the days with what we want?

It is not by accident that both poetry and prayer rise out of stillness, as both are the function of deep listening. So don't try to get anywhere when you write or when you pray. Simply still yourself and listen, and soon—in time—the Mystery will begin to speak to you through its thousand disguises as life on Earth.

Like all young writers, I resisted this in favor of a dream of fame. I worked very hard to create something great out of nothing. Only to exhaust my dreams and finally listen. Then, the poems came. Then, the books came. Then, unasked-for connections dropped in front of me like rain.

When young, I searched for my voice, never realizing what I searched with was my voice. Older, I wanted vision, never realizing what I looked with was vision itself. Now losing track of quests and years, I just want light, which between people is simply love. Now I realize that wanting light is a form of light, and wanting love is what makes Earth turn to the sun. So fundamental that we don't even see it, so elemental that we call it "physics" and look for love elsewhere.

*The gift of deep silence is that it allows us to let go of
what we want so we can receive what we have.*

An Invitation to Listen

- As you move through your day, listen for one detail
  through which life is speaking to you. In your journal,
  describe what carries this one detail. Then tell the
  story of finding this detail to a friend. After describing
  what carries the detail and telling your story of finding
  it, write the detail's story in the voice of a character.

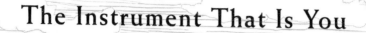

The Instrument That Is You

*The more faithfully you listen to the voice
within you, the better you will hear it sound
outside. And only he who listens can speak.*
DAG HAMMARSKJÖLD

What Is Voice?

The reward for working hard and long at being thoroughly human is that you begin to discover and inhabit the instrument that is you. And the gift for being an instrument is threefold: we are at last of use, we help repair the world, and we are played like a reed by the wind. Against all odds, being an instrument lets us carry truth and give away tenderness. When so deeply engaged, we become finely tuned beings. And despite our wildest ambitions, there can be no greater destiny than to convey the larger Universe through the truth of who we are.

Given this, how do we understand voice? Great jazz musicians each have a singular voice, uniquely theirs, *and* they each convey the eternal chord of all music. Likewise, a person's voice is their singular quality of expression through which the eternal chord of all life is conveyed. In the same way, a writer's voice is at once singular and universal, encompassing much more than style. For voice resides at the place inside where the personal expresses the Universal.

A writer can't create voice, only make space for it by being authentic and tend to it when it comes through. Walt Whitman's voice was that of a hawk gliding endlessly over a growing city. Rainer Maria Rilke's voice was that of a shaman draping a sacred hood over everything ordinary so he could watch it glow. And Emily Dickinson's voice was that of a small bird perched on a window ledge between the body and the soul.

Let me offer three more ways to further understand voice.

First, consider the banks of a river. The banks don't own the river. They carry it. The more thoroughly the banks hold the river, the deeper the river flows. The deeper the river flows, the more hollowed the banks become. Until the river runs faster and deeper, carrying the silt of the river bottom with it. Like the banks of a river, we are hollowed out by life to carry the deeper current to a greater sea. In just this way, the instrument that is you is beautifully hollowed by the deep waters that you carry. And while no one owns what flows through them, that phenomenal depth carries the silt of who you are with it. In time, we become like the banks of an old, swift river and add to the flow of life without ever owning it. The sound of all-that-is flowing through us is the sound of our voice.

Next, consider a flute played by the wind. As wind will blow through a flute propped on a hill, all-there-is will sing through us when we can stand firmly in the open. As we experience moments of Oneness, the wonders of living ring true as they move through us. At that point, the currents of the world enliven our voice. Yet how do we become such a flute? Along the way, we are hollowed by experience until we learn how to accept life by letting go. Then, when empty and in the open, I arrive—through exhaustion or shedding—at that place where I can speak nakedly without inhibition, like Adam or Eve, with nothing between me and the experience of living. With nothing in the way, the sound that comes from deep within me is my voice.

Finally, consider a tuning fork. Earlier, I mentioned that being a poet is mostly about being an awake human being, which in turn is mostly about living each day as a tuning fork in the midst of life's currents. When we can be true to our own nature, we receive the underlying tones of life. They vibrate through us into the world. When true to life, our voice becomes a tuning fork intoning the Sacred.

Day by day, we're called to listen to life through the instrument of our own life. This requires an ability to follow the scent of life-force wherever it goes rather than trying to direct or bend life-force. I remember meeting with the Jungian analyst Helen Luke toward the end of her life. She had taken me under her wing. One afternoon, over tea, she circled a paragraph of my writing and said, "This is unlike you." I leaned closer and said, "What do you mean, Helen?" She poked her finger at the paragraph and said in her British accent, "Ego (*aa-go*)." I was taken aback as I didn't think the passage was self-centered at all. She tapped her finger at the paragraph again and continued, "You're directing the material here, instead of listening to where it wants to go. That's ego (*aa-go*)."

To know our voice, we need to let life move through us and honestly express what that movement makes us think and feel. Then, we have a chance to sing the world into being, one utterance at a time, not by preaching or persuading but by listening to life and each other, the way a flag listens to wind.

A writer can't create voice, only make space for it by being authentic and tend to it when it comes through.

An Invitation to Explore Voice

- In your journal, explore what voice means to you. Then, listen for a metaphor for the nature of voice as you understand it. Detail the metaphor in a poem about voice.

- In conversation with a friend or loved one, describe a musician or writer you admire who has a singular, yet universal voice. What is it that makes their voice singular? What is it that makes their voice universal? What does their voice convey to you?

The Quarter Turn

I suddenly knew I was looking at it from the
wrong angle and I gave the cloth in my hand a
quarter turn. Immediately I saw a beautiful and
coherent golden pattern. . . . In wonder, the pattern
had emerged, to be seen in all its beauty by those
who could learn to make the quarter turn.

HELEN M. LUKE

I mentioned Helen Luke in the last chapter. This chapter holds another deep learning from her. The above quote is from Helen's inner autobiography, *Such Stuff as Dreams Are Made On.* She begins the book with a dream in which one of her oldest friends, now gone, is asked on the other side to weave a tapestry that tells the story of her life. But as Helen looks at the cloth, it makes no sense—until she gives the cloth a quarter turn and the pattern of her friend's life emerges plainly.

Helen then offers the quarter turn as a synonym for a paradigm shift, as a way to understand those unexpected shifts of perception that return us to the hidden wholeness, the spot of grace, the Oneness that exists beneath all subjects and conclusions. And like the fine-adjustment knob on a telescope or microscope that brings what you're looking at into focus, the quarter turn is the skill of perception by which you can bring into focus the instrument that is you.

We have all experienced shifts in how we see. It is not something to teach, but to lift up and share, to understand better, and to enlist more fully. If we want to see together, we have to understand how we see as individual spirits first.

I experienced a profound quarter turn during my struggle with cancer. I was at one of many frightening ledges, needing to make another impossible decision. The tumor on my brain was pressing, and I had to say yes to surgery or chance waiting for further tests. Then, on October 4, 1987, we had an early, heavy snow in the midst of autumn's full color. I woke that morning, tense and afraid of what lay ahead. When I looked into our yard, I saw that the early storm had brought all the trees down because the leaves, no matter how brilliant, had weighed the trees into snapping. If the leaves had let go, the snow would have left the trees standing. This was a paradigm shift for me, which caused me to see holding on and letting go differently. I stopped trying to maneuver my way through my cancer and began to grow slim as a leafless tree.

In the 1996 movie *Phenomenon*, starring John Travolta, car mechanic George Malley sees a flash of light on his birthday and begins to experience extraordinary moments of far-reaching perception. The first of these sudden perceptions is a quarter turn. George is planting a small vegetable garden in his backyard, which has been plagued by a rabbit nibbling at all the stalks. George has tried everything to keep the rabbit out, from building a mesh fence to putting the fence deeper in the ground. One night, he wakes with a sudden start and quietly opens the gate to the garden. Then he waits on his porch and watches. After a while, the rabbit shows and leaves the garden under the moonlight. Sure enough—the rabbit wasn't trying to get into the garden but trying to get out!

Sometimes, quarter turns defy any logical connection. As a young man, the poet Stanley Kunitz writes of being at a crossroads in life, needing to decide whether to devote himself to poetry and all that poetry points to or to pursue a more stable career. He was walking in a Pennsylvania field at dusk when, beyond all reason, he saw some geese sweep across a mottled sky. Intuitively, he knew the geese were saying yes, and he knew what he had to do.

When author Donald Miller asked the novelist Toni Morrison how she had become a great writer, he wondered what books she had read and what method she had used to structure her practice. She laughed and said, "Oh, no, that's not why I'm a great writer. I'm a great writer because when I was a little girl and walked into a room where my father was sitting, his eyes would light up." Sometimes, the gleam in our father's eyes is a quarter turn.

Two legendary quarter turns involve a saint and a scientist. The story of St. Paul is an archetype of the quarter turn. Saul was a persecutor of early Christians until a moment of revelation knocked him off his horse, and he rose as Paul, a devout follower of Jesus. Here, the shift in seeing brought something entirely new.

And Sir Isaac Newton's legendary experience of an apple falling on his head opened him to the understanding of gravity. Here, the quarter turn allowed Newton to see what already existed. His shift in seeing brought what was always there in view.

In his searingly honest poem "New Heaven and Earth," D. H. Lawrence has a paradigm shift that is a personal awakening. It seems the very act of facing himself is the quarter turn by which Lawrence realizes that he has been so self-centered and self-possessed that "[When] I kissed the woman I loved, God of horror, I was kissing myself."

In turn, he admits that "I was so weary of the world, I was so sick of it, everything was tainted with myself." By the end of the poem, he is born anew, unsure of what is next, except that it is now real. This is the transformative power of expression, that unto itself it can be the quarter turn that can render us more vulnerable to the Mystery.

Sometimes, quarter turns grow within us like seeds. During my cancer journey, I recalled being a boy of six or seven chasing a butterfly in a reservoir. When I finally caught it, I felt it flitting in my cupped hands, and it became clear that as long as I held it, I couldn't see it. To see it, I had to let it go. When I did, its lightness and magnificence circled me. I quickly forgot the lesson. Until thirty years later, when overcome with fear that I would die. Then, at last, the quarter turn came back to me. I realized that the fear thumping in my chest was like the butterfly cupped in my hands. As long as I kept the fear inside, I couldn't see it. And so, I tried to let it go, so it could mix with the quiet magnificence that was speaking to me when I was so close to death, so close to life.

At the end of his life, the painter Raphael Soyer said, "I wish I had more eyes." The only way to have more eyes is to stay open to the view from all of life's positions. When we fall down, we must see from there. When lifted beyond our hopes, we must see from there. And when we fall down again, we must not forget the view of the lift. And when we are lifted again, we must not forget the view of the fallen. No one view is complete or permanent, and so, no one view is home. It's the place from which we see that is home.

This is the transformative power of expression, that unto itself it can be the quarter turn that can render us more vulnerable to the Mystery.

An Invitation to Examine a Quarter Turn

- In your journal, explore a quarter turn
  that you have encountered.

- First, describe an experience, event, or
  relationship that changed your way of seeing
  an important issue or problem. This is the
  trigger or catalyst of seeing differently.

- Next, describe how your lens of perception
  shifted regarding the problem because of
  this trigger or catalyst. This is the actual
  shift in seeing that occurred in you.

- Finally, describe how this new seeing enlarged
  who you are and how you see the world. What
  did the shift in seeing lead you to?

- Go back and highlight one phrase or line in
  each of your writings: one for the trigger or
  catalyst of seeing, one for the shift in seeing
  that occurred, and one for how your vision
  enlarged. This is your quarter-turn haiku.

- In conversation with a friend or loved one,
  discuss your personal quarter turn, describing
  the trigger or initial catalyst, the actual
  shift in perception that took place, and how
  your vision or understanding has enlarged.
  Then read your quarter-turn haiku.

The Inner Critic

During this period of development [Rodin] was undisturbed
by any voice from without. There reached him neither
praise to mislead him nor blame to confuse him.
RAINER MARIA RILKE

Consciousness is a great gift. But like all gifts, there is an underside, which in this case is self-consciousness. At some point, we internalize the praise and blame that surround us, until we tip over the edge of just being aware and present, and begin to watch ourselves. This watching of ourselves pulls us out of direct living. The Argentinean poet Jorge Luis Borges names this self-consciousness the watcher, who in time becomes our inner critic. Our work is to deepen the gift of our consciousness while limiting the impact of our inner critic, keeping the self-watcher at arm's length.

It is natural to want to improve, to work toward excellence and mastery of what we love. But at some dark edge, we can slip into the reaches of what-is-not over the improvement of what-is. Then the inner critic begins to measure all we do against an impossible standard, and we in turn begin to live in the breach.

I'm thinking of an early Zen parable about a master calligrapher who is asked to design the signage to the entrance of the city of Kyoto—a great honor. He enlists his best student, now a teacher himself, to aid him. The student criticizes every attempt by the master, wanting to ensure that what the master offers is worthy of this honor. The master is particularly frustrated because it is he who empowered this critical sensibility in his best student. Finally, after a day of criticizing, the student leaves. Once alone, the master consults the authority of his own soul. He closes his eyes and in one stroke brushes the perfect signage which now stands above the entrance to Kyoto.

The press of the inner critic is ancient and deep. For there is something bottomless about our striving to please, which cannot be satiated, only set aside. The meditation practices from all traditions recognize this and ask that we enter silence long enough that the inner critic has nothing to grab on to. If we are still enough, long enough, we can disempower the voice of the inner critic by accepting the completeness of things as they are. I've come to believe that we must move through this struggle with our self-consciousness in order to find and inhabit our true voice.

In that struggle, there is a direct relationship between the power of our inner critic and the strength of our self-acceptance. The less we are able to accept ourselves and our humanity, the more dominant our inner critic. The more we can accept our light and gifts and place in the world, the less dominant our inner critic. So, when feeling pressed by your inner critic, better to assess the condition of your self-worth than to try to satisfy your critic's demands. This becomes a recurring practice: the discernment of how insecure we are in our being and what steps will restore our foundation of worth.

Eventually, if we stay true to the work and to our role as a conduit for the work, we get out of our own way and arrive at a place of inner congruence. As the Abstract Expressionist painter Hans Hofmann said, "At first, you paint with everyone in the room. Then, you paint with only you in the room. Finally, you paint with no one in the room."

Under all our ruminations and self-recriminations, we breathe the poems in our heart of hearts as we meet each other and the world. We do this deeply and constantly, regardless of how we judge ourselves. All this to say that you are a poet already. It's in the quality of your being. The rest is a manifestation of this basic quality.

Our work is to deepen the gift of our consciousness while limiting the impact of our inner critic, keeping the self-watcher at arm's length.

An Invitation to Speak to Your Inner Critic

- In your journal, describe how loud your inner critic is these days. Is your critic at arm's length or closer? Then take your current situation and write your own parable about the inner critic.

- In conversation with a friend or loved one, discuss how your inner critic shows up, and tell the history of your inner critic, including your earliest experience of unhealthy criticism.

- Later, in your journal, begin a conversation with your inner critic, describing what a healthy relationship with that critical voice might look like.

Diving Down and Coming Up

I always felt that it was an unconscious process. Rather than writing the songs, I'm just the first person to hear them.
JAMES TAYLOR

Divers learn straight away not to enter or rise from the deep too fast. Or you will get the bends. You may even rupture your lungs or heart. This is also a law of physics for the inner world. Any depth worth entering will not allow you to race through it. For diving down and coming up requires a slow courage, so the taste of the deep can be absorbed into your very being by the time you step back into the world. This is part of the craft of being a poet: diving down and coming up.

It is only later, after the dive, that all the work with words begins. For after the dive, the poem is already written in your being and you must squeeze your heart like a sponge onto the page, rearranging its feeling and insight before the water from the deep dries.

The sweet Irish poet John O'Donohue speaks to this process when he says: "The poet wants to drink from the well of origin . . . [but] the poet must reach deeper inward; go deeper than the private hoard of voices down to the root-voice."

Yet we must not skip over the private hoard of voices but work through them like a diver swimming through the tangle of seaweed growing out of the bottom. Until you reach into the soft, timeless sand for what you think is a small treasure, only to realize it is the peace of slipping your tired hands into the untouched bed of Mystery that is the treasure. And wanting to bring that presence back into the world, you surface empty-handed. But with that presence on your fingers, you go to the page or touch the face of someone you love who is struggling. After such a dive, to watch the page glow or your friend or lover go calm—this is the true gift of poetry.

Again, we are returned to this theme: through the personal, we discover the Universal. Going to the bottom of my heavy box of memories, I discover the bedrock of all memory. Going to the bottom of my personality, I discover the well of all personality. Going to the bottom of my soul, I discover the underground spring of all Spirit. In this way, discovering voice has to do with discovering presence. And diving down and coming up is another mysterious friction that shapes the instrument that is you, refining your voice as you enter the deep and return to the world.

In truth, we cannot avoid the particular and run to the general and still have heart. We cannot avoid the loose stitch in our wound and run to the suffering of humanity and still have compassion. We cannot avoid the knots in our relationships and run to the broken net of social justice and still keep our care intact. Only by diving down into our own humanity, troubled and tangled as it may be, can we strengthen life on Earth.

I had a great teacher in all of this, though I spent very little time with him. He was the remarkable poet Stanley Kunitz, who died in 2006 at the age of 100. Others knew him better and studied with him longer. Through his work, it was clear that the longer he lived, the more he became a holy poem himself. He once defined art as the "chalice into which we pour the wine of transcendence."

I remember a time, almost twenty-five years ago, when he came to the University of Albany, where I taught. He read in a hall to about three hundred of us, his soft rhythmic voice boring below our masks, giving rise to the one place we all swim in. When he finished, a young student raised his hand and asked, "How long did it take to write that poem?"

I will never forget how he started to answer, and then, as if distracted by the voice of an angel that only he could hear, he peered off above us for what seemed like minutes of silence. He returned to the crowd and answered, "My whole life."

With that, he made me realize that as we only see a dolphin when it breaks surface, because it spends most of its life out of view in the deep, so it is with the poet and the artist and the lover aching to be loved. Stanley was such a dolphin breaking surface before us that night. His confessing as much affirmed the truth that we are all poets and artists and lovers. He made me realize that even when silent in the deep, we are writing poems and birthing art and loving. And more importantly, the poem is writing itself before breaking surface through us, as the love is writing itself into the souls of the world wanting to love.

The beauty of it all is that though the gesture of life breaking surface like a dolphin stuns us, none of this—not the poem, the painting, the music, or the act of courage or love—is possible without the labor that takes place out of sight in the deep. Down there, living and poetry are one, and love and courage and frailty are one. In truth, everything that matters grows out of view in the deep. And the diving down and coming up is the art of living—never sure where we will break surface next.

Diving down and coming up requires a slow courage, so
the taste of the deep can be absorbed into your very
being by the time you step back into the world.

An Invitation to Dive Down
Where You Are

Enter this exercise three times during the next two months:

- Find a quiet place where you won't be distracted, and enter that space slowly. Concentrate on your breathing without any intent until you have a sense that your mind, heart, and body are moving in rhythm with your breath. Then begin this guided meditation.

- Once centered in this quiet place, walk outside in silence for at least thirty minutes and follow what you are drawn to—a branch, a tree, a smell, an expanse of water, a bird song—and welcome it as your immediate teacher.

- Now settle and listen deeply to this small teacher and seek its guidance on the following set of questions, journaling that dialogue—all in silence.

  What question about life is present in your days?

  What obstacle is challenging you most right now?

  What is that obstacle trying to teach you?

  How is that obstacle addressing your central question?

Love Your Window

Of the many windows we have into life, it is through the window of our eyes that we take in the vastness of experience. Through the window of our mind, we take in the endless patterns that help us understand the web of life. And through the window of our heart, we feel the thousand ways we are affected by other life, the thousand ways we are each other. So it is imperative that we love our windows and care for them.

We take for granted that eyes look out, but they also look in and are also see-through, letting light fill us as well as letting light come forth from us. Our ability to see is a window both ways—into the unseeable terrain of spirit and outwardly into the reality of the world. Poetry is the trail of what moves through us both ways. The music of what moves through us is another way to understand voice.

In the last year of her life, my grandmother, who was ninety-four, was strong and weak by turns. She was living in Kingsbrook Medical Center in Brooklyn. I went to see her on a beautiful day in May. When I entered her room, she seemed glum. I said, "Grandma, what's the matter?" She shrugged and replied, "It's a grey day." At first, I thought she was wandering, not quite lucid.

I looked around her small room, and the only window she had was covered with dirt. I said, "Grandma, the window is dirty. We'll have it cleaned. But for now, let me wheel you into the courtyard. It's so nice out."

She looked to the caked window and with the knowing chuckle of someone who had lived almost a century, she said in her thick Jewish-Russian accent, "Got a dirty eye, see a dirty world."

For sure, there are grey days, but what Grandma taught me is that before you brace yourself to meet a dark day, make sure that your window isn't dirty. I can't tell you how many times this chuckle from Grandma has saved me. In coping with reality, it's important to clean the window of your eye, the window of your mind, and the window of your heart before charging forward.

Love, honesty, and expression are what clean the window of our heart. And each time we inhabit love, honesty, and expression, we *thin* the window between in-here and out-there a little more, and this thinning between our inner world and the outer world brings us closer to life.

It's also important to clean both sides of your window, for experience films the inside of your window, too. This effort to clean our windows of perception is an ongoing practice. It's known as introspection, another way that you can care for the instrument that is you. The continual practice of introspection opens a deeper embrace of reality, as the goal is not to get dirty or to stay clean, but to stay as alive as possible by meeting experience and staying clear.

It's easy to fall to one extreme or the other. When obsessed with experience, we make a god of getting covered with reality. When obsessed with staying clean, we make a god of purity. The truth is that we can't escape either. Experience films our window, and love and introspection clean it, over and over. But every time we clean the window of our eye, our mind, or heart, we gain an inch of wisdom. This is how wisdom is earned. We get covered with experience and then we clean our lens by working the inner life. This too is the reward for a life of expression.

There is one other type of window to speak of—a truth window. In a cob house, an ancient type of dwelling built of mud, clay and straw, there's always a wall that has a truth window. This isn't a window to the outside, but an opening that shows what the wall is made of. This is the window of transparency.

There are always two windows to care for: our window on the world, which opens both inwardly and outwardly, and our truth window, which dares to show what our walls are made of. The question I leave you with is: How will you care for your windows?

The continual practice of introspection opens a deeper embrace of reality, as the goal is not to get dirty or to stay clean, but to stay as alive as possible by meeting experience and staying clear.

An Invitation to Know Your Window

- In your journal, describe your favorite window, inner or outer: where it is, the first time you came upon it, why it is your favorite, and what it has shown you. Then describe the kind of window *you* are and what others might see through you.

- In conversation with a friend or loved one, ask them to describe their favorite window. Later, create a poem or story about the importance of windows.

Part 3

The Deeper We Go

By giving our full attention to whatever is before us, we can stay close to what is sacred. Toward this end, we have to understand the nature of practice, so we can be awake enough to feel the patch of wind pressing on the chickadee's throat. Toward this end, we have to develop our own practice of holding nothing back, so we can be alive enough to feel the delight of someone who was blind who can suddenly see. And so, this part of the book explores how we can create and inhabit a lifelong practice of listening, expressing, and creating.

Yet no one can teach you how to do this, though we can compare notes. No one can listen for you, though we can soothe each other with our attention. No one can give voice to what comes through you, though we can find a thousand ways to say, "I love you, I love this life, I love the power of life to inform all the things I can't see."

The deeper we go, the more we realize that we are each part of an endless search. It may or may not lead to great accomplishments, but when we can educate the heart, we are very close to everything we need.

Breaking Surface

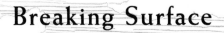

Let no one keep you from your journey . . .
You are the only explorer.
Your heart, the unreadable compass.
Your soul, the shore of a promise
too great to be ignored.

MN

The Endless Search

As soon as we are born, we are part of an endless search that really goes nowhere. But it's the journey and movement of the search that enlivens us. The great Hindu sage Ramana Maharshi said, "There is no greater mystery than this, that we keep seeking reality though in fact we are reality."

It is through this endless seeking that effort reveals grace. It is through the endless search that life moves through us until we realize that heaven is wherever we are, if we meet life completely with an open heart.

And just as moving through water keeps fish alive, moving through life brings our indwelling presence into the world. Moving through life allows meaning to accumulate through relationship. As some fish swim with no destination, we arrive with a yearning that has no destination, a search that keeps us alive, despite the thousand places we think we need to go.

But we are not fish. And as no one can survive the ocean without a vessel to carry them, even the sea of Spirit will drown us if we don't create vessels to carry us. A fundamental purpose of creativity is to engage us in the creation of vessels that will carry us in the sea of Spirit, in which we need to immerse ourselves to make life meaningful. My poems and books are the boats that carry me, that keep me close to the deep where I am most alive.

Inherently, will and surrender are the oars that steer the soul, workable gifts that return us to the heart of what matters. And along the way we are drawn into the search for whole-mind thinking, which is revealed through the life of metaphors; the search for belonging, which is revealed through the life of stories; and the search for authenticity, which is revealed through the life of poetry.

The search for whole-mind thinking reflects our inborn urge to regain Unity. And nothing brings the Wholeness of Reality into view more than the life of metaphors. For the more we see, the greater our chance at experiencing wisdom. And the more we feel, the greater our chance at experiencing compassion.

Each soul is a cell in the bloodstream of humanity and, as such, each soul is indispensable to the health of life. For without healthy cells, there can be no bloodstream. And without a healthy bloodstream, there is no place for cells to live. This is a metaphor that evokes whole-mind thinking.

A covenant that appears for being on the endless search is that we become committed to the art of putting things together. In the 1600s, the Japanese master Basho spoke about this to his student Kikakou:

> We shouldn't abuse God's creatures.
> You must reverse your haiku.

Not:

> a dragonfly;
> remove its wings—
> pepper tree.

But:

pepper tree;
add wings to it—
dragonfly.

The world depends on which way this thought unfolds. The metaphors we come upon lead us to whole-mind thinking, which reminds us to put things together rather than take things apart.

Our search for belonging is brought forward through the life of stories, as narratives are the threads that bind us. Once we know a person's story, we tend to experience kinship over separation and to offer praise more than blame. I'm thinking of a woman I know who after the death of her lifelong friend was drawn to wear her friend's sweater when all alone in the afternoon. She slowly began to feel the one long story of women who were friends throughout the ages. She closed her eyes and began to feel the clothes and jewelry they all had shared.

I'm also thinking of being nine and watching my father in his basement workshop carefully building a model sailing ship, so immersed in using a tweezer to set the miniature rigging that I could sense the story of everyone who ever built a sailing ship in the quiet of our basement.

Or when I was in the Jewish Cemetery in Prague, watching an old man put his hand heavily on a family stone. Though I didn't know the details of his loss, I stood close enough in silence to share in his mourning, and felt the endless story of loss and mourning reverberate around us. Stories of belonging restore our sense of kinship.

I'm often asked about the difference between my efforts in poetry and prose. In poetry, I have always searched for metaphors that reveal how everything is connected, how everything is informed and enlivened by the same Source. The further I go, the more I realize that in writing prose I'm taking those inscrutable, compelling metaphors and I am *entering* them, living with them, being in relationship and conversation with them, trying to retrieve and unfold the logic of Spirit nested within them. This is the basis for the spiritual nonfiction that I write. This is what rises in me when I try to release in prose what's carried to me in poetry.

Finally, there is the search for authenticity, which is the bedrock of all our searching. For no matter where we go, none of it matters unless we are real. And poetry is the chief means of discovering and expressing authenticity. Because poetry offers us a direct way to live in truth. The poetry of authenticity can connect us to the wholeness of humanity and the mystery of the Universe at any time in any way. Poetry is the honest record of our days.

I'm thinking of the time in Washington Park when I saw an elderly man staring off into Eternity. Having seen me see him, he came over and sat beside me, and asked, "How can we go there together?" That question changed my life. Or the time I saw a homeless boy in South Africa, begging with such dignity that it made me explore all the ways my heart has been broken open through the years. Or that time in the hospital after having a cancerous rib removed from my back, when the doctor suddenly came to remove the tube that had been siphoning blood from my lungs. Sitting at the foot of my bed, my dear friend Paul jumped to my side so I could hold on to him. That moment uncovered the essential step we all must take if we are to love. These were authentic moments that revealed the poetry of life.

Ultimately, you can grunt your truth and it will still be beautiful. For the deeper sense of beauty is the shine of authenticity more than the aesthetic qualities that stun us. No matter how awkward, our authenticity is the foundation of lasting beauty. If someone coughs "I love you," it's more beautiful than an unfelt love sung in perfect pitch. In the same way that no one can quench your thirst by drinking for you, drinking of life directly is the only way to stay essential and substantial.

A covenant that appears for being on the endless search is that we become committed to the art of putting things together.

An Invitation into Whole-Mind Thinking

- In your journal, take a metaphor, one you've read or discovered yourself, and describe the whole-mind thinking it draws you into.

- In conversation with a friend or loved one, tell a story that demonstrates our struggle to belong. Later, weave the story you have told into a story that you write.

- In your journal, write a poem about a recent moment of authenticity you found yourself in.

Venetian Interior

If it doesn't come bursting out of you in spite of everything,
don't do it. Unless it comes unasked out of your heart and
your mind and your mouth and your gut, don't do it.
CHARLES BUKOWSKI

In my late twenties, I entered a hall of paintings by John Singer Sargent at the Clark Art Institute in Williamstown, Massachusetts. Along the back wall was a long, dark painting of a room called *Venetian Interior*. It drew me immediately.

In the painting, a middle-aged woman was sitting with her hands on her knees. She looked forlorn. In the upper-left corner was a small window. The light bursting through that window insisted that the street outside was filled with sun. At first, I was drawn to the forlorn woman staring at the floor, but once brought into the world of the painting, the focal point was the sunlit window. In fact, the subject of the painting was the world of light *outside* the painting. I instantly wanted to be on that street, to leave that room. The painting pointed to a reality beyond itself. The subject of the painting was a world beyond its frame.

The only traces of light in the room were a splash of light on the woman's ring and on her knee. The painting was a metaphor for the dark room we can fall into, even though we know there is light all around. The painting illustrated the truth that the miracle of life doesn't stop because we've lost our way in the dark.

I was enthralled with the effect of this scene and stood there for almost an hour. Sargent had given me an image for my work. I've always wanted my stories, metaphors, poems, and books to point to the intangible mysteries that live outside their frame. An essential purpose of art, no matter its form, is to bring what's invisible and unseeable into view, however briefly. I believe the work of a poet is to be a threshold to the larger world of light that waits beyond our rooms.

A crucial paradox of poetry is that the only things worth writing about are those that can't be said. We simply create a window that points to the light that exists beyond its frame. Buddha said to his students one evening, "My teachings are just fingers pointing to the moon. Be sure to look at the moon." All insight and art are fingers pointing to the larger Unity of Life.

It's interesting that light is only visible by what it illuminates. Light travels millions of miles from the sun with no trace until it enters our atmosphere and lands on the things of the world. Though the source of light in Sargent's painting is bursting outside the dark room, it moves through the room unseen until it illumines the woman's ring and knee. Her life waits for her to stop staring at the floor and to see the traces of light that touch her, so she might look to the window and then to the world outside her room.

This is the journey from difficulty to Wholeness that each of us faces, regardless of the dark room we create or fall into. The gift of all mystical art is that it serves as a window to the world that exists beyond our frame. And so, regardless of its craft or excellence, a great piece of writing or art or music serves as a window between the Unity of Life and the reader, viewer, or listener sitting in their room.

I was discussing this with my dear friend Don, who is a master watercolorist. He told me of the time he saw Michelangelo's *Pietá* and how it made him cry. In that moment, the *Pietá* was the window of light connecting Don's personal history of being held with the river of all compassion bursting through the window that the statue opened. Don then talked about how seeing a homeless, sickly dog in the street had the same effect on him, connecting his own sense of frailty with the river of frailty that was bursting through the window of the dog's wet eyes. We began to see that any moment of authentic living is like Sargent's window of light, insisting on the Unity of Life that is always present beyond whatever personal room of mind or heart we find ourselves in.

In the deepest sense, moments of art are more than the words or the paint or the notes the pianist plays. Moments of raw, true living are the windows of light that insist on the Unity of Life that is always beyond our particular situation. And when wholehearted and present, each of us is an artist. Our feelings are the colors and our authenticity is the brush.

We all know the presence of light by touching what it illuminates, in ourselves, each other, and the world. This is why seeing a burst of sun on the beak of a chickadee stops us. Because through the window of the illuminated chickadee, we somehow feel and see the history of light and song. This is why seeing a burst of tenderness in the eyes of a stranger makes us tender. Because through the window of that tenderness, we feel and see the history of tenderness. This is why talking like this with my dear friend Don opens us to the truth of all we can't say. Because through the work of honest friendship, we feel and see the ground of being that spills through the lighted window of our heart, our eyes, and our mind. The spilling of light into us and out of us is the function of art and poetry.

An essential purpose of art, no matter its form, is to bring what's invisible and unseeable into view, however briefly.

An Invitation to Point to the World Outside Your Frame

- In your journal, describe a piece of art or writing that, like Sargent's *Venetian Interior*, points to a world outside of its frame. Look at this closely and record, as best you can, how the artist or writer creates this effect. Later, write a poem or story that has a similar effect.

A Word about Effort

Regardless of what's produced or created, being immersed in whatever is before us while holding nothing back brings us alive. Giving our all allows us to discover that grace waits at the end of effort. Often, I find that effort is revelation in slow motion.

Over the years, I've learned that the difficulty of the path has no bearing on the quality of the work or what is learned. I now experience the writing journey as a climb through different forms of terrain. One day, we're led through an open meadow in the light, the next through a patch of landslide where the path is covered with old stones, each with a story. This takes longer, as each stone has to be overturned and listened to for its story. I've learned to keep moving at the pace of the path, no matter how it unfolds. Later, I can shape and order what I find.

I thought, at first, that real, lasting work—whether building a barn or writing a poem—was a matter of honesty. And it is, and so there is no choice but to find the skill to do it cleanly. But I have learned that essential work is not even feasible unless one is immersed—unless in the midst of discovery one is patient, exhaustive, and determined to keep things honest overnight, through winters and lazy moons. For in a world where we are pressed to be quick, timely, catchy, where acceptance and celebrity loom as the soft addiction of our culture—in such an industry of filling emptiness—it requires courage and perseverance to stay authentic and to pursue your depth, your spirit, your truth—for months and years and, possibly, for the rest of your life.

It seems almost impossible to counter the age we live in, but our enduring testaments lie under all our noise: dormant, waiting to be created, waiting for sustained crisis and attention to release them. Waiting for unmitigated effort, the way Virgil worked *The Aeneid* for ten years, though he exclaimed along the way, "I'd rather die than look at it one more time." The way Lorenzo Ghiberti took twenty-five years to carve the bronze *Gates of Paradise* for the doors of the Baptistery in Florence—a quarter of a century to sculpt bodies in relief so real they seem to have been breathing just moments ago, then dipped in molten gold. Unmitigated effort, the way Friedrich Schiller, on his deathbed, kept his feet in iced buckets in order to stay awake to finish his play, *Mary Stuart*. Effort, the likes of John James Audubon who, after years of live sketching in the woods and swamps of America, brought more than seven hundred drawings of North American birds to England. There, his monumental book *The Birds of America*, which appeared as individual prints from 1827 to 1838, included more than 435 hand-colored, life-size prints made from engraved copper plates.

It seems a challenge today to stay in love with the unknown, to stay confident and secure with what we *want* to know. It seems imperative to keep our faith in our pursuit of aliveness, long after everyone else goes to bed, gives up writing, changes jobs, stops keeping in touch. Most real dreams don't come true because the dreamer doesn't outlast the novelty of initial dreaming, the way most relationships today don't survive because it's so much easier to fall in love than to stay in love.

My own failed attempts have led me to the bedrock of my soul through such unexpected openings. From here, I can offer that it is the sedative of unworthiness that tries to quiet us from our gifts, that has us worried about trying too hard when few of us have ever tried hard enough.

Essential work is not even feasible unless one is immersed—unless in the midst of discovery one is patient, exhaustive, and determined to keep things honest overnight, through winters and lazy moons.

An Invitation to Engage Effort

• In your journal, take an image, story, feeling, or question, and apply your sustained effort in exploring it over the next month. I encourage you to create an ongoing narrative and to research the images and stories that arise, to be in conversation with others, and to re-enter your stream of inquiry again and again, without forcing a conclusion. Stay in the stream of what you're learning, recording what you understand along the way.

• In conversation with a friend or loved one, describe one way you might enter the effort of staying in love more than falling in love. Likewise, describe how you might enter the effort of living one of your dreams rather than dreaming it.

Giving and Getting Attention

A poet is one who notices, or causes notice and
places a gentle breath at that place of notice.
PUANANI BURGESS

Not Great but True

Yesterday I was clever, so I wanted to change the world.
Today I am wise, so I am changing myself.
RUMI

There is an ongoing tension we each face between giving attention and getting attention. Giving attention steers us back to Center. It opens the vitality of the Universe and brings us back into the stream of Oneness. Giving attention is connective. On the other hand, getting attention is a form of drifting from Center. If attention comes your way, well enjoy, but cultivating it and seeking it is paddling away from Center. Getting attention is deceptively isolating. It ultimately leads to being seen but not held.

At the core of it, giving is often more crucial to our health than getting. Giving attention is life affirming. It's how we attend things. For inner health is often restored when we honor the need to recognize and verify. Somehow, this validates our experience and connects us to the world. However, getting attention is how we are attended to. It seems our yearning for approval drives us to be recognized and verified. Here, being seen somehow relieves our angst about being insignificant, at least temporarily.

For many of us, getting ahead requires getting attention. Too often, once that place is secured, we are still getting and no longer giving, and the whole process becomes self-defeating. In time, we learn that giving attention is how we get a heart.

In my own journey, it has always been a thorough attending of life that opens me to a wonder that compels me to write it down, as a way to enter life further. But early on, feeling insecure, I was admonished by my own insatiable need to be seen, telling myself, "You must get ahead as a published poet." Soon, the way an Olympic hopeful does his laps, I was addictively going to the mailbox daily to withstand the faceless rejections, searching quietly and desperately for the one small yes that would confirm that I existed—all this while the wonder waited for my return.

Too often, once on our way, the momentum of getting keeps us from giving, and we resurrect the wrong kind of power. It can happen to anyone. The confusion between giving attention and getting attention is so great that we often want to be well known rather than well knowing. We often want to be great rather than true. We often long for celebrity while secretly aching for something to celebrate.

Because all young people are taught to be ambitious, I began as all young artists do—working toward some imagined greatness that might reveal itself in time if I could stay devoted enough to my craft. But along the way, I was humbled to be more uplifted by what was true rather than what was great, by what was heartfelt rather than what was intricate. It kept me close to my own experience, which when entered honestly began to reveal the common ground of all experience and all time.

From there, I risked more by entering the poems than by writing them, not sure where they might go, and found myself touched and changed by showing up in my life so completely. Well, that's not very different than being changed by loving another, is it? Now in the second half of life, I am devoted to being in that holy space where the conversation of aliveness exists. It's not about the words but the poetry of life that is revealed and enlivened by our honest engagement.

The process of writing and expressing—whether you become a writer or not—offers many valuable tools for living. If you concentrate on learning what those tools are and are diligent in using them, this concentration of wakefulness will help you live, and chances are that you'll surface good writing.

Ultimately, we need to focus on seeing, not being seen, on verifying and not being verified, on clarity and truth rather than producing beautiful art. Too often, young writers want to create and write themselves rather than give voice to what they are experiencing. A Thomas Merton quote that has helped me in this regard is, "Eyes were not meant to see themselves."

In all honesty, I can affirm what you already know, that once you've lived the work and done the work, you are the work. And going public with the work is about casting seeds and seeing which will sprout in the world. Regardless of which seeds come up or not, the truth we serve drips like medicine beyond our dreams and needs, as when it reaches the mother who lost her daughter just in time to revive her belief in life. Each time we give our full being, a small miracle issues forth beyond our control.

So, when feeling the pain of being lost or insecure, when alone and out of touch with all that matters, give your attention to anything, quickly and fully. And the Universe, which has always been near, will come rushing back to fill you.

For many of us, getting ahead requires getting attention.
In time, we learn that giving attention is how we get a heart.

An Invitation to Better Understand Attention

- In your journal, describe which dominates your time: giving attention or getting attention. Explore why. Whatever part of you needs attention, how can you use your life-force to give attention to yourself?

- In conversation with a friend or loved one, share a story about giving attention and where that led, and a story about getting attention and where that led. Later, write a poem or story about giving and getting attention.

Staying Close to What Is Sacred

The highest reward for a person's toil is not what
they get for it, but what they become by it.
JOHN RUSKIN

The original definition of the word *sacrifice* is "giving up what no longer works in order to stay close to what is sacred." The understanding this definition rests on is that while everything is always sacred, what keeps us close to what matters will change—because we change. And so, an inner practice is needed to put down what no longer works in order to find what will work now.

What this means in the life of a writer is that we have to return to a beginner's mind and heart, no matter how accomplished or comfortable we feel in what's brought us this far. What is exciting and revelatory today may harden into a confining habit that we are fearful to put down. We have to be ready for our way of expression to change and evolve. Though he had other failings, this was perhaps Picasso's greatest gift, his courageous pursuit of the next form. He moved steadily through the years from realism to his Blue Period to cubism to abstract sculpture, all with a vigilance to stay close to what was calling him.

Beyond art, this call to stay close to what is sacred is how we grow as beings in bodies in time on Earth. For while the soul within a self stays constant, the self does not. This is the dynamic of transformation that no one can resist. While my essential vision and voice have remained constant my whole life, I am not the same person I was thirty years ago. Nor do I write the same way.

It is our sincerity and commitment to growth that leads to great work. And great work is that which connects us and transforms us in the retrieving and expressing of it. In describing the original ethos of haiku, the essential three-line form of Japanese poetry, the scholar Stephen Addiss tells us that:

> Sincerity . . . is more important than mastery. [And] brevity, directness, naturalness, simplicity, and allowing the [reader] to participate are the most important qualities. True [haiku] does not invite comments like "What a great [poem]!" as much as "How delightfully the [reader] and the poem interact!"

Hamada Shoji was a twentieth-century master potter in Japan known for throwing large, striking bowls. His process of quickly pouring glazes from a ladle, followed by a few strokes of a brush, took only a matter of seconds. He was natural and delightful, and above all, sincere. Demonstrating his swift and peerless technique to a group of British artists, one remarked that he thought it inappropriate that glazing a monumental work should take only fifteen seconds. Hamada kept working and replied, "It took sixty years and fifteen seconds to create this work."

By staying simple and direct, Hamada Shoji stayed close to what is sacred, whether that meant working large or small, or quick or slow, even in the creation of the same bowl.

A jazz master is a good example of someone who has made an art of staying close to what is sacred. After years of discipline and focus, the pianist or saxophonist will master the keys and valves of their instrument with such ease that there is nothing between hearing the music and playing it. Being such a conduit is the height of improvisation, which requires the hard-earned facility of playing chords and notes seamlessly, so that the musician can open their heart directly to the music that is heard.

For a writer, the interface of words and the page are our instrument, our keys and valves, and the abundance of story and image is where we need to listen with our heart. Until there is nothing between what we see and hear of the Universe and our hard-earned facility in writing it all down.

In 1794, the mystical poet William Blake self-published his prophetic collection of poems, *Songs of Innocence and Experience: Showing the Two Contrary States of the Human Soul*. Blake summoned tremendous courage in writing about ideas of passion and energy contrary to the values of his time. He also displayed courage in following his imagination to scribe the poems by hand, embedding them in his own paintings. No one had mixed writing and painting like this. Though he intended for the words and the painted images to be inseparable, universities have pried Blake's work apart for centuries, studying his poems in English classes and his painting in art classes. Only recently are we able to see the art and the poetry integrated as he intended. And none of his work would be known if he didn't have the courage to self-publish and be who he was everywhere.

A hundred years later, Joseph Conrad began his daring, classic novel *Heart of Darkness* as a three-part serial that was published in the London journal *Blackwood's Magazine* (February, March, and April 1899). But what he tripped into was vastly larger, deeper, and more troubling than a magazine story. Bravely, he kept pursuing what he heard beyond the expectations of his editor, only to discover that he was swimming in the vortex of human impulse and emotion. He wasn't sure what this all meant but stayed committed to retrieving this dark and powerful narrative.

Whether called to the heart of our darkness or the songs of our innocence, both Conrad and Blake stayed close to what is sacred by following what seemed most true, even when those around them thought their work strange. While we need to question our conclusions, *where we land*, we always need to enter what calls us, *where we begin*.

Mythologies throughout history are filled with blind soothsayers who turn from the glitter and seduction of the world to whisper the song-lines of a deeper, timeless sense of being that has always endured. Often, their mythic blindness represents the strength of spirit we are each born with to withstand the noise and tumult of the world. In the face of the hypnotic pull of success and chaos, we can stay close to what is sacred by listening to the unwavering soothsayer within us.

By whatever form or content possible, it is the writer's responsibility to expose the glitter and seduction of the world, while revealing and affirming the song-lines of our deeper being. It is the writer's noble obligation to show compassion for how we suffer the noise and tumult of the world while loving the unwavering soothsayer that lives in each of us, until our deeper being walks freely among us.

By whatever form or content possible, it is the writer's
responsibility to expose the glitter and seduction of the world,
while revealing and affirming the song-lines of our deeper being.

An Invitation to Stay Close
to What Is Sacred

- In your journal, describe a time when you gave up some way of being, thinking, or feeling that no longer worked in order to stay close to what is sacred. How did you know this way was no longer working? How did you put it down? What new way has taken its place?

- In conversation with a friend or loved one, discuss some area of learning that is calling you and how you can explore it further. Later, write a poem or story about following a calling into the unknown.

Pulling Threads

A story or poem may reveal truths to me as I write it.
I don't put them there. I find them in the story as I work.
URSULA LE GUIN

I want to speak about a particular way of listening that being a poet has taught me through the years. As the years wear the faces off statues and the crests off warriors' shields, I have been worn of the lines between what is visible and invisible, what is objective and subjective, what is real and imagined. I can no longer distinguish between the life of poetry and the poetry of life. Thankfully, everything is real!

Now, I walk down a street in summer, and moments glow and call. Each holds all of the Mystery, the way one drop of ocean contains the entire ocean, the way one small act of love contains all the feeling of everyone who's ever loved.

The task now is to slow down enough and be present enough to enter each moment that calls. For each enlivened instant—the sudden light on a crow's beak as it pecks the ground, or the shadow that covers the sad girl's face as she stares into her half-eaten sandwich—each is a thread in the fabric of the Universe, each imbued and teeming with Spirit and wisdom. The task now is to be humble enough and attentive enough to pull the threads. When I do, without fail the threads unravel the cocoon of my own making that shrouds me from the Mystery that is always present.

Who would have guessed? Nothing is wanting but we in our want. Nothing is fragmented but we in our isolation. Nothing is completely dark but we in our hesitation. It turns out that the Universe—the endless fabric of now, the weave of all life that is timeless—is the one and only subject. And listening for it, to it, with it, we are privileged to become glowing threads ourselves. All of us here to unravel each other and to love back together what we find.

We are left with the beautiful chance to spill our presence into the world. For each of us has a particular piece of wisdom, a bit of Eternity that if not brought forward will be lost, or at least stay silent during our time on Earth. This piece of inner wisdom that is in everything doesn't have a name. We could call the piece that resides in you your soul. So, as you would honor a grandparent or teacher, how will you befriend that in you which has no name? What kind of relationship will you have with the oldest part of your life, so it might speak to you?

Let me tell you how I try to make sense of my own experience. Two things I'm sure of are that we gather meaning through relationship and that we understand life by working with what we're given. This applies to creative work as well. I've never imagined my books as outlines to be filled. Once complete, not one of my books has ever been the book I started. Like everyone else, I move through the days, stopped by wonder and pain, and by worry and surprise. With each stopping, I listen for the story, the insight, the question, or metaphor that is my next teacher. As I travel to be in learning circles, I find that speaking to the honest questions I'm asked causes thoughts and associations to surface that I didn't know I knew. So I pull the threads and save them in order to listen to them and work with them later. After months—of listening and speaking, when alone and with others—I have pages and pages of fragments, rough-cut gems that I have to work with to understand their meaning.

Then I take the questions that won't leave me alone and turn them into possible chapters. Next I reflect on all the fragments that have risen from conversation and circumstance along the way. And based on what I hear from each, I place them like shards or beads into the chapter files. Months later, I dump all the shards and beads from each chapter like rough pieces of mosaic before me. Then I hold them and put them together like chipped stones or riddles I have to decipher. In this way, the light on a tree in Vancouver three years ago and a quote from a little-known painter I discovered last month rub against the breathing of my father in his last days. And in the crucible of a patience that's always hard to sustain, the meaning imbedded in each heart-instance starts to reveal itself. This is when my work as a poet truly begins: in weaving the things I could have lost over time into the fabric of what matters. I'm always humbled to retrieve insights and patterns much greater and more useful than my small mind could have imagined. As the conversation of a lifetime keeps unfolding, I uncover meaning.

Regardless of what you do for a living, the only important vocation is listening to the heart when it says: *this is vital, this is alive, this can't be lost.* For me, the vitality and aliveness always precede my understanding of them. Making sense of our experience demands a faith in knowing what matters before we understand what it means. Making sense of what we gather demands a conversation with what we've found and with what has found us.

Describing how Eudora Welty retrieved her fiction, Ronald A. Sharp recalled:

> She puts bits and pieces of stories or novels in a file, and when she is ready to start shaping the material, she spreads out the scraps of paper on a bed or a table or the floor, so that she can see it all in one place, and then she actually "pins" together the various pieces into a whole.

In speaking about improvisation, the great jazz vibraphone player Stefon Harris said: "There are no mistakes on the bandstand. What is a mistake? Many actions are perceived as mistakes only because we don't react to them appropriately."

Discovering as we go, there are no mistakes, just more of the fabric of the Universe coming into view. I used to think that pulling threads would lead me somewhere, to a pot of meaning on the other side of the hill, or to the center of time where the gears of existence would shine and grind. But pulling threads has only taken the coverings off of everything, including my efforts. And all unraveled, I found this poem:

Incandescence

I have worked months
on lines like these.
But I am not these lines nor
the effort to shape them.

Now that I have written books
I find I am not a book.
Now that I have sung
bouquets of song, I confess
I am not the song.

Now that I have loved,
I discover that what I am
shows itself to be touched
but is not the touch.

Even when feeling the wind
blow aside the veils
I cling to,

even when loving
the instant of seeing,
I am not what is sighted
nor the instant it is seen.

Undressed of all there is to do,
I vanish in a gesture
that is everywhere.

This is when my work as a poet truly begins: in weaving the things I could have lost over time into the fabric of what matters.

An Invitation to Practice Pulling Threads

- Over the next week, note in your journal one detail from each day that stands out and speaks to you. Describe each carefully. Then, wait a few days and return to the details you have gathered and weave them into a poem or story.

- In conversation with a friend or loved one, discuss a small thread you pulled and followed and what it led you to.

Travel and the Writer's Mind

My good friend Jacquelyn Vincenta is a novelist and essayist with a penetrating sensibility. She was traveling in Lithuania, about to begin her novel, *The Lake and the Lost Girl*, when the landscape and people of Lithuania called to her strongly, and she began writing about the presence of where she was. The following email conversation happened between us in the spring of 2011.

Jacquelyn: My days in Lithuania are winding down. Three months of travel drawing to a close and my mind has started to turn homeward.

I have a question for you in relation to your own experiences. Does it make any sense that while I have been here I have felt reluctant to let down some guard to fully engage my imagination and heart and write? It has been so strange. I feel I have soaked up and written down notes and notes, letters, and journal pages. I have photographed, watched, listened, and all in all been present. If I was on a mission of experiential quest—my soul and senses gathering what bits they can, in spite of my own lumbering, shadowy interior ghosts—I feel I have been successful. But the processing has been put off, the resistance to it huge, and I don't understand why.

Perhaps you have thoughts on this.

Mark: Oh yes, I have experienced this sort of cross-purpose. Perhaps you're not supposed to process all this yet. Perhaps you're being asked to take in more. I find that when I push, nothing happens, and so I need to keep taking things in, to stay in conversation with life, and when the time is right—things flow very easily. I encourage you to not see the shift as some failing on your part but more the appearance of unexpected currents in a river as you ride down it. Our intentions while necessary are only guesses. Our challenge is to respond to the landscape we find ourselves in once the map blows away.

In terms of resistance, I find that I often try to mentally process or synthesize material when the only true way to access the already-put-together-whole is through the heart. And so, I must let my heart focus on whatever detail it can't let go of, follow that detail, be in conversation with it, and write from there.

We're often held hostage by our own design of what we hope to write and how we hope to write it, when the soul will speak what and when it wants. A deep part of the writer's call is to drop our designs and follow what we see and hear—in real time.

The story of how a book has come to me—and is still coming to me—bears sharing. In my late twenties, I had a vision to write a book called *Spiritual Ecology*, based on exploring dynamics of the plant world as metaphors for our life of being. I began with enthusiasm and gathered so much. In the midst of this, I discovered a great deal about self-pollinating and cross-pollinating plants. I was intrigued to learn that cross-pollinating plants are known in the world of botany as "out-crossers." But I couldn't find what self-pollinating plants were called and so went on a long search, which took me to unexpected places.

One day, lost in the stacks of the SUNY–Albany library (this was before digital archives), I found quite remarkably that self-pollinating plants are known as "selfers." I immediately knew that this compelling analogy, between selfers and out-crossers, was the basis for an entire book. But what of my *Spiritual Ecology* book waiting for my return?

I wound up leaving that book under construction and for eight months feverishly explored this one analogy, which kept unraveling and opening up into another book that I finished, called *While We Are Blossoms*. I still have *Spiritual Ecology* in mid-creation all these years later, and I hope to return to it. For a long time, I thought I was neglecting it but came to realize that each book has its own gestation, timing, and labor. And who knows, perhaps the whole purpose of *Spiritual Ecology* was to lead me to *While We Are Blossoms*.

So, I encourage you not to resist the shift but to go with it. At the same time, I also encourage you to meet whatever inner resistance you are feeling to this material by opening your heart to its many details and staying in conversation there.

I leave you with a recent poem, called "Loosening." Trust your voice. Trust your muse. Trust the ways-you-are-not-yet-versed-in, which all this is calling you to meet. The reward for doing things well is not that we get to keep doing those same things well, but that we are invited to meet new things in new ways.

Loosening

On the plane, I woke with a start and
spilled water on my journal. The pages
curled. The words blurred. And last week,
it happened again. I hung up the phone
and tipped the cup. It seeped under the
blotter on my desk, softening all my lists
and numbers. And yesterday, in the
thunderstorm, when the sky was spilling,
I thought I heard a whisper. This morning,

I brought my plate and cup down the stairs
carefully, our dog by my side, when I caught
Buddha smiling in the mirror, floating like
someone waking after a hundred years.
Of course, I've been annoyed by all this
spilling. But I think it's telling me
that I'm ready.

Jacquelyn: The level of specificity, synchronicity, and bounty in the Universe's interaction with me over the last three months is unbelievable. The way I have been swept along in this journey, as if there was in fact some plan, not my own, that was drawn up somewhere that I can't see. The currents, yes, are the perfect metaphor, and they have not only been powerful but so harmonious with each other. The spiritual path has completely flooded the production path I had in mind.

Of course, I hoped to see, to remain open, to be in fact more creative in this situation, away from everything at home, longing for the sort of break that can allow patterns to shift. But I did expect to follow, more or less, the intellectualized plan I had in mind.

I saw the breaking away, the journeying, and the time here as a situation that might allow some openings in my heart, in my stuck way of experiencing things. I could never have dreamt that Life would be so prolific with its messages, lamps, anonymous hands, and voices along the way.

Even the brokenness and grief I kept facing internally, facing the Nothingness and Unground of Life in Vilnius without a buffer, gave way to an intensity that kept leading me to meditation, to walking, to action, to writing.

But the writing has been from eye to hand to page. I have felt almost afraid of wandering off the path of detail. It has helped me feel attached to my days, my hours, my world, in spite of the lingering notion that I was alone in a strange land. Honestly, I have not been able to hold to my map. You are right, it has blown away. It's been astounding how much more intimate the alternative journey has been.

Yesterday, on my walk, I suddenly came upon a five-hundred-year-old Franciscan church with its massive doors open, candles burning, and one woman praying. I paused, for I too do something like pray because I am never quite balanced these days. I walked on and attended a chamber music concert given by four sisters in an old building downtown. At the last minute, in walked one of the Franciscan monks from that church, prayer beads on his belt. He shuffled to the seat beside me as if assigned and sat down. His presence was peaceful. We both sat still through the intermission, though I thought I might leave. The girls continued and at length finished, then sang a song without instruments—an old melancholy Lithuanian ballad that felt like it was rending my heart.

I meditate nightly with my own prayer beads, and here the beads somehow walked into the concert with the monk. So I carried the song, I carried the monk, back through the dark streets, wrote notes in my apartment, where I stopped trying to think. I looked at my hands, not wanting to disturb the moment, and floated in the dark with my mala beads. They have now gone with me up to the dream workshop on the Baltic coast, where I washed them in the sea, and then to the countryside where I washed them in the river and tied linen thread to them.

But because I am someone without much of a past regarding myth, religion, or ritual, I am taking each step carefully: watching, listening, walking more. Every day has been like this. It probably looks like ease, vacation, play, but it feels like work that requires constant attention and energy.

Whether it is ego wanting to hold to some plan or project, or my fear of the future, or my fear of living a life without definition, or whatever comprises that in me which worries about what I do and do not write, it is undeniable that I gave up my usual resistance to the unknown and to other ways of knowing during this time here.

I have literally been living as if every day is a shamanic journey. I have no idea yet what this means in terms of the writing. But in the way you have trusted what speaks to you, I find myself with no other choice but to do the same. I am sure that I would not trade this weird, difficult journey for five hundred pages to edit at home. And yet, I have been drawn to turn to writing in a way that I have not since I was twenty.

Mark: What you share here is a profound affirmation that you are being led into the poetry of being in which life through its vital specificity reaches out to love us and wrestle us to live more deeply in the world. This is a thousand times more life-giving than the efforts, no matter how noble, to willfully extract poetry out of nothing. I have found that the greatest single evolvement in my own creativity these past five years has been to have more faith in the innate order and structure of things-as-they-are. And so, I've been working at letting go of my need to create an architecture and structure for books and simply work more completely at discovering and inhabiting the divine structure that is everywhere, if we can clear our minds and hearts to perceive it. Then, as you are feeling now, it's all a matter of entering what-is and taking heart-notes. This requires another level of trust. Now I look for ways to enter this new, old place where I have never been, eager to see what it has to teach me.

I find that when I push, nothing happens, and so I need to keep taking things in, to stay in conversation with life, and when the time is right—things flow very easily.

An Invitation into the Mystery of Travel

- In conversation with a friend or loved one, ask them to tell a story of travel, sharing what they had hoped for, what they had planned for, what actually happened, and how they were changed by this journey.

- Later, in your journal, write a parable or story about a journey that changed the one on the journey.

Stacks of Wheat

*I am certain that children always know more than they
are able to tell, and that's the big difference between them
and adults, who, at best, know only a fraction of what they
say. The reason is simply that children know everything with
their whole being, while we know it only with our head.*

JACQUES LUSSEYRAN

It is humbling and inspiring that the Impressionist painter
Claude Monet worked a lifetime to hone his ability to see,
only to paint his masterful water lilies through double cataracts
as his very practiced way of seeing was breaking down. The
aging painter's devotion to keep painting what he saw models
a courage that is necessary if we are to wrestle into view the
mysterious resources that remain essential and largely out of
view. The truth is that we can't know where our fierce practice
will lead us. Our best work waits to be realized beyond our
most stubborn intentions. Repeatedly, we must give our all to
render reality as clearly as possible, especially when we don't
understand what is happening. And then, to listen to what the
battered angels of time will thunder into our being.

I spent a month staring at Monet's works: the stacks of
wheat, the many versions of the Rouen Cathedral, the plein-air
canvases of Etretat on the northwest coast of France, and his
ethereal water lilies. He kept circling the repositories of light,
often painting the same scenes at different times of day, like a
scientist measuring the effects of light.

But more than anything, I was deeply moved by Monet's
fierce and steadfast attention. One night I dreamt I was in

conversation with Monet. He stroked his long beard and said, "I've come to trust the beauty already present in whatever I am looking at. If I am faithful enough in my attention, I don't have to make my renderings beautiful. Attentive enough and my paintings will carry the beauty already there."

Finally, I attempted a poem, trying to convey all this. It's called:

Stacks of Wheat

So many thought Monet
was making it up,
imagining wildly
what things might be
if God held them closer.

But what he did
was much braver.
Like a human microscope
he kept looking and looking
as warmth left the trees
as waves remade the sea
as loss slowed into peace
undoing hard men.

He watched
strange flowers open
where only silence had been.

He focused so far in
that everything shimmered.
He proved by the strength

of his attention that
nothing can keep
light out.

It's a small leap
to say that love
works this way—
a light that lives in the bones,
just waiting to be seen.

So why not
prop your heart
out in the open
like the easel that it is
and dab its blood
on everything.

The truth is that no one creates in a vacuum. We create in partnership with all of life, stirred by one particular thing at a time. The residue of the life that surrounds us informs our choices and guides our urge to create. For example, in 1930 Picasso bought the Chateau de Boisgeloup forty-five miles north of Paris and turned the horse stables into a sculpture studio. His first carvings, thin and horselike, were whittled from branches found on the forest floor. And I imagine that the vitality and muscle of the horses that had lived there—running through that forest, their beautiful heads snorting the cold autumn air—I imagine these vital energies guided his hands, without his knowing, as he molded the figures in white plaster that became known as the Boisgeloup sculptures.

When small fragments are held, life-force will show itself. If we are attentive enough to grasp this, it will lead to a dynamic form of expression. Often, a poem will present itself through a very unexpected particular detail that stops me, that calls to me, that draws me into greater conversation with life.

Last fall, I was driving the back way home, eager to work, my mind racing with the unending list that we're always behind on. Just then, the morning sun filtered through the beautiful fall leaves, bringing my eye to the softness of a small deer. From there, my eyes went to the space between its lifted hoof and the orange-covered ground. It took the list from my mind. At least for a while. I pulled over and felt like I'd entered the world beneath the world, the one we're always chasing, though it's always wherever we are. I felt the entirety of existence in the light between the doe's hoof and the ground. I took an impression of the scene in my heart and thought I'd write it down later. But I stopped again, less than a mile down the road, and scribbled the following poem on a napkin. It was a moment of underlying connection that confirmed for me that we are, against our will, reduced to joy, worn to who we truly are. I knew at that moment that this was the final poem of a book about joy.

The poem I wrote that day is the title poem of my book *Reduced to Joy*:

Reduced to Joy

I was sipping coffee on the way to work,
the back road under a canopy of maples
turning orange. In the dip of woods, a small
doe gently leaping. I pulled over, for there
was nowhere else to go. She paused as if

she knew I was watching. A few orange
leaves fell around her like blessings no
one can seem to find. I sipped some
coffee, completely at peace, knowing
it wouldn't last. But that's alright.

We never know when we will blossom
into what we are supposed to be. It might
be early. It might be late. It might be after
thirty years of failing at a misguided way.
Or the very first time we dare to shed
our mental skin and touch the world.

They say, if real enough, some see God
at the moment of their death. But isn't
every fall and letting go a death? Isn't God
waiting right now in the chill between the
small doe's hoof and those fallen leaves?

If any of this speaks to you, then go outside and wander and
listen and wait. Let life know you are looking for connections.
Let others know that you are ready to learn. Don't hide your
eagerness to be touched by the fragments of the world. Collect
their small histories and let them join with your own.

*Our best work waits to be realized beyond
our most stubborn intentions.*

An Invitation to Look and Wait

• When you can, go for a walk by yourself in silence. It
  might be in the woods, or by the sea, or in the city.
  Walk slow enough that you are looking with your heart.
  Be aware of the details that seem to glow. Follow one
  and sit before it, noticing what you see opening there
  as well as within you. Like Monet, don't try to create
  something beautiful. Just give your full attention to
  the truth of beauty that is before you. Record what
  you are experiencing, both outwardly and inwardly.

• A week later, read what you have written to
  a friend or loved one, and describe your
  experience. If they are willing, go on another walk
  together and see what life has to offer you.

Understanding Practice

We think we practice for the game, to apply what we learn
in the future, but the reward for our covenant with practice
is that it delivers us into the ever-present river of Eternity.
And any instrument of immersion will do, until the practice
dissolves and we blossom into a moment of authentic living.

MN

Placeholders

As a boy, my father introduced me to the sea. Something about it was his home. It held him and received him. He would sail on it for hours, days—weeks if he could get away. It was on that boat that I first saw the sun glitter up the sea. That sheen hypnotized me, as if the back of some luminous creature was just under the surface about to show itself. I thought if I could enter the deep, I might meet that luminous creature too big to name.

The sheen of the sun on the sea befriended me. But, being called into the world, I would forget about the sheen, and the enormity of the sea, and the endless dependability of the waves—until the noise and tumble of the world would send me back to the sea. Then, when exhausted, I'd walk along some patch of surf where the clouds would part and the sun would glitter up the sea again. And I'd remember, as someone waking from a long sleep, I'd remember all that is out of view, all that we stand on, all that holds us up.

When teaching creative writing at SUNY–Albany in my late twenties, I shared the worst image I ever came up with, calling that sheen of sun on the sea, "liquid tinfoil." Though the image wasn't right, I told my students that I used it as a placeholder, a visual bookmark that would bring the irreducible sheen of the sea back to me. This is the power of symbol and metaphor. Regardless of how rough or precise, the images point to what is clear and unsayable, so we can remember and revisit what has meaning.

This morning, some forty years later, I'm again by the sea, and the sun is high, the clouds are few, and there the familiar sheen glittering up the sea—old guide, old friend. And still, after a lifetime, I can't describe it or name it. I can only feel it.

I keep relearning that what matters is unsayable. And yet, every attempt to reveal it helps us live, the way every seed grows by reaching for a light it can't see or name. God is such a sun. Truth is such a sun. Love is such a sun. And each of these—God, Truth, and Love—is just a temporary name for something too big to stay named.

I only know that to be alive and to gather meaning from living, we're asked to throw our words and feelings and questions, like wood, onto the fire of all that's unsayable—to keep the shimmer of what matters before us.

And whether you write poetry or stories, whether you write at all, we each have a need for placeholders that let us return to the things too big to name but too important to forget. While the placeholders we discover and articulate are very personal, they help connect us to what we have in common. We all need to work with symbols so we can return to the larger order of things of which we are a part.

I keep relearning that what matters is unsayable.
And yet, every attempt to reveal it helps us live.

An Invitation to Discover an Image

- In your journal, locate one aspect of life that defies being named and try to create an image that serves as a visual placeholder for it. On three different occasions during the next week, write and speak this image as a way to bring the ineffable aspect of life that it represents back into view. Spend more time with the original aspect of life and see how it touches you. Each time you do this, revisit your placeholder and refine the image.

- Later, in conversation with a friend or loved one, discuss the process you've just experienced in your journal.

When the Work Comes Alive

There are certain stanzas—sometimes entire poems—
whose meaning not even I know. It's what I do not know
that holds me still. You were right to ask. . . . But
I don't know, I tell you. . . .
But even these add to our lives.

YANNIS RITSOS

When the work comes alive, the best we can do is get closer to it, keep in touch with it, and trust its inherent meaning. One of the hardest things to teach young writers is to follow the work wherever it leads. Often, we have a dream or vision and set out to blueprint it and then write our way through the blueprint. But when the work comes alive and takes us in another direction, we think we've failed. When characters refuse to fit our image of them, when plots go off on their own, and when a want to speak about the beauty of life winds up as a dark complaint, the work is co-creating with us. It's as if the invisible essence of what you're poking at sees your sincerity and says, "Now that I see you're serious, I'll show you what this is really about."

This is why it's important to never be lulled into thinking that you are in control. In graduate school, a good friend of mine—a talented novelist of great integrity—had spent four years unfolding a generational story, replete with character histories, all set in the Midwest. After all that work, he came to me one evening, glum but determined. I asked what was wrong. He stared past me and said, "The story has run into a dead end. At first, I thought all my work was for nothing. I was devastated. But I know in my heart that this was the path I was supposed to follow. So, I kept looking at the hundreds of pages I had written, pleading for it to speak to me."

I was in awe of what he said next. He sighed and dropped his shoulders, and went on, "But all this work, all these pages, all this time—it's all been an excavation to the real beginning, which I didn't know I was digging for." He put his hands on his knees and gathered his resolve and continued, "Well, I can insist on forcing the novel to go where I have imagined. Or I can accept that it all has led me to what's real. Both paths are hard. So why not follow the one that feels true?"

Within a week, he started over. And in five more years, he published the novel that was waiting under the novel that led him there. When the work comes alive, it's because we've demonstrated our dedication, and the change of direction is our reward if we can get past the disappointment of our will.

My own experience of this process led me to this lyric called:

The Poems

When starting out, I was so excited
that anything showed up, I thought
I was done. But somewhere along
the way, I realized they are alive
and I wasn't wrestling them into
view. They, respecting my effort,
agreed to be seen. Not to be revealed, but to be loved. Now I
circle back in the morning to see
what they need from me. Just more
of my attention which starts with me

undressing what I know. For the
longest time I thought I was revising.
It's more a conversation in which I
keep learning how to listen. And
when I do, they will after a time
pull aside a cloth or cloud to make
obvious the reason they have come.

I have to confess that my understanding of revision all
changed after almost dying from cancer in my thirties. Now I
ask myself every day, "If all I have is this one day, will I revise
something I've already lived or live something new?"

Given this, will I strive to revise my expressions to 99 percent
of what is possible or leave them at 85 percent or 90 percent and
go on living? Is that extra percent of refinement worth the life-
force it would exact from me? I am committed to making every
expression as clear as possible, but now it is out of a commitment
to being a conduit for truth and not for the ambition of creating
lasting art.

Given how precious life is, I affirm, day after day, that what
I'm listening for and then saying is more important than how
it is said. Now, when I revise, it is out of a devotion to what is
retrieved, not because I'm striving for flawless writing. I still
go over things several times in great detail, but as a way to stay
in love with what I've seen, not because of an obsession with
excellence. I keep clarifying what I find, rather than trying to
polish and perfect the artifact of words before me. Now I go
over things out of respect for what can't be said. Since respect
means "to look again," my effort is to make my attempts as
clear as possible, not to fashion something extraordinary.

And so, I am not interested in perfected writing but holistic
writing. My life's work has been a devotion to praising, bearing

witness, and exemplifying, wherever possible, a totality of vision and feeling regarding the Unitive Mystery of Life. Therefore, after I'm gone, I do not want any of my writing edited or altered from how it is found—whether these pieces are finished or in draft. I have been revisiting and tending these works continually, even those in progress. All to pay tribute to the overall process of expression rather than the polished veneer of any one piece.

Through the years, I have been blessed to work with a few exceptional editors, but for much of my life, I have faced well-intentioned editors who, under the guise of economizing language, have limited the scope of vision and feeling I have been exploring. I would rather leave flawed, far-reaching expressions than more perfect, guarded artifacts.

All of this to affirm that the creative process is alive and messy, no matter the order we try to ascribe to it. And no matter how surprising and disruptive the unfolding of true expression is, I've learned that, when stuck, I need to withstand the urge to anoint my insecurity and remember that the work is alive and calling. Then, in time, I will humbly ask of the work itself, "Now that we've finally met, where do you want to go? What would you like me to do?"

When the work comes alive, it's because we've demonstrated our dedication, and the change of direction is our reward if we can get past the disappointment of our will.

An Invitation to Go Beyond Your Intent

- In your journal, describe a time when the unfolding
  of something you were writing—a story, poem,
  or essay—changed direction on you. How did
  you respond? What is the difference between
  what you intended and where the piece took you?
  How have you been changed by this journey?

The Monkey and the River

When people are at a loss, the guide ferries them over.
When one is (awake), one ferries oneself.

HUI-NENG

The simplest and hardest thing to do each day is to be here—fully, completely, without turning away. There's a story I love about a master who sends his apprentice to meditate by a river until he's learned all the river has to say.

The apprentice is earnest and devoted. He spends several hours finding the right place to sit. At first, he sits very near the bank, but all he can hear is the rush of the river. He's too close. Then he moves to the top of the hill overlooking the river. Now he's too far. Finally, he settles midway beneath a willow. He sets out his special blanket and sits on his special pillow and begins to meditate. Quickly, he dozes off. When he wakes, he feels guilty to have wasted time. He strains to focus and tries even harder.

After three days, the apprentice is exhausted and has a terrific headache. Just then, a monkey happens along and jumps in the river, splashing and yapping and hooting. This cracks the apprentice who begins to weep. Not sure what has happened, he gathers his things and returns to tell all to his master. His master sighs and puts his hand on the young man's shoulder and says, "Ah, the monkey heard. You just listened."

Sometimes, we get so lost in our practice and devotion that we forget that the goal is to get wet. There is much we can learn from watching, but observing at its best enlivens us to participate. The aim of watching the river of life is to join the river of life. Likewise, the goal of expression and writing in particular is to enter what the words point to.

In the 1600s, the legendary Japanese poet Basho spoke about the mystery of deep listening in this way:

> Go to the pine if you want to learn about the pine, or to the bamboo if you want to learn about the bamboo. And in doing so, you must let go of your preoccupation with yourself. Otherwise you impose yourself on the object and don't learn. Your poetry arises by itself when you and the object have become one, when you have plunged deep enough into the object to see something like a hidden light glimmering there. However well phrased your poetry may be, if your feeling isn't natural—if you and the object are separate—then your poetry isn't true but merely (accurate) counterfeit.

The reward for entering life so completely is that we become one with the life before us. The authenticity of poetry leads us to this union. As a cancer survivor, I'm compelled to extend Basho's wisdom to the realm of healers by casting his thoughts this way:

> Go to the ill if you want to learn about suffering, and to their spirits if you want to learn about truth. And in doing so, you must let go of your preoccupation with yourself. Otherwise you impose yourself on the patient and don't learn. Your diagnosis arises by itself when you and the patient have become one, when you have plunged deep enough into the patient to see something like a hidden light glimmering there.

However well phrased your diagnosis may be, if your feeling isn't natural—if you and the patient are separate—then your diagnosis isn't true but merely (accurate) counterfeit.

When we watch from the outside and think we are on the inside, we are misled into a prison of false living, where our insights might be accurate but counterfeit because we have refused to enter the life we are watching. This subtle but deadly distance between us and life can form a film over our understanding of life. This mental distance is exacerbated in our age by the flood of reality TV through which we vicariously think we are living while only watching others live. The honest life of expression is a timeless antidote for watching. It brings us closer to the hidden light glimmering in all things.

Our understanding of practice deepens with a constant pledge to enter life more fully. We learn to open our eyes in order to see, and we learn to open our heart in order to love. To do this, we need to watch but not to make a home of our watching. At some point, we may even need to retreat from the world in order to be in the world, the way a chick matures in an egg in order to be born. In this way, the awakening of our soul is an apprenticeship that leads to the practice of being kind and useful in the streets.

The honest life of expression is a timeless antidote for watching. It brings us closer to the hidden light glimmering in all things.

An Invitation to Enter More Than Watch

- In your journal, write a poem or story about someone who watches life and how they are prompted by love or suffering to enter life.

- In conversation with a friend or loved one, describe a time you watched and a time you joined, exploring the difference as you experienced it.

The Practice before the Practice

There is always a practice before the practice; a sitting before the incomprehensible long enough to feel and sometimes understand the Mystery each instrument and craft is designed to invoke.

In Japan, before an apprentice can clay up his hands and work the wheel, he must watch the master potter for years. In Hawaii, before a young man can ever touch a boat, he must sit on the cliff of his ancestors and simply watch the sea. In Africa, before the children are allowed to drum, they must rub the length of skin stretched over wood and dream of the animal whose heart will guide their hands. In Vienna, the prodigy must visit the piano maker before ever fingering a scale, to see how the keys are carved and put into place. And in Switzerland, legend has it that before the master watchmaker can couple his tiny gears, he must sit long enough to feel the passage of time.

Starting this way enables a love of the process that is life-giving. The legendary cellist Pablo Casals was asked at ninety-two why he still practiced four hours a day. He smiled and replied, "Because I believe I'm making progress."

It is this sort of deep progress that saves us.

While there are times we need to discover the path as we go, more often it helps to pause where we are and take in as much as we can, so the Whole of Life can refine our eye and heart. Then, we see different possibilities and make different decisions. You can work long, hard hours with a dull tool or stop and sharpen your instruments. In just this way, we can work long, hard hours with a dull mind or a calloused heart. Or we can pause to sharpen our mind and refresh our heart. These efforts to be clear and touchable are part of the practice before the practice.

There is an old story about two brothers whose father dies, leaving them a riddle to solve en route to their inheritance. Their father's will says, *The treasure I leave you waits beyond the edge of what you know, when you can put down what you see and follow.*

The older brother was certain that this meant taking a journey into the wilderness. So he left home to journey to places he'd yet to experience. The younger brother was certain that his father's riddle meant undoing his assumptions about life to this point. So he retreated inwardly into the wilderness of silence, where he could journey to the unmapped territory of his being.

Both brothers journeyed in their own way for years. As the older brother kept looking for what was missing, he grew weary and bitter. But the younger brother, in time, let go of his father's treasure, and began to see everything about him as a treasure.

The brothers in this story represent the parts of us that search inside and outside for what matters. Our challenge is to look to the bottom of what-is rather than to keep searching for something we think is missing. Otherwise, we will grow weary and bitter for the search.

Inevitably, we all take turns seeing and not seeing, searching inside and outside, and being sharp and dull. It is the practice before the practice that helps us regain our aliveness when the hardships of living batter us.

The great Chilean poet Pablo Neruda speaks to this in his masterful poem, "Poet's Obligation":

> To whoever is not listening to the sea
> this Friday morning, to whoever is cooped up
> in house or office, factory or woman
> or street or mine or dry prison cell,

to him I come, and without speaking or looking
I arrive and open the door of his prison. . . .

So, through me, freedom and the sea
will call in answer to the shuttered heart.

When we commit to this life, we take turns being conduits for freedom and the sea. When we commit to each other, the practice before the practice lets us look before we act and ask before we answer until we apprehend the Whole. But it is humbling to remember that we all move between not listening and listening. On any given day, we can feel cooped up or spacious. At any moment, we can feel shuttered or free. At any moment, we can separate further or complete each other.

Our challenge is to look to the bottom
of what-is rather than to keep searching
for something we think is missing.

An Invitation to Personalize the Practice before the Practice

- In your journal, identify a skill or craft you feel called to and describe it. As the Hawaiian must watch the sea before sailing in a boat, what would it be like for you to pause and take in the Whole of Life before engaging in the skills of this craft? Take the time to do so, and see how the Whole of Life informs your understanding of this craft.

- Later, in conversation with a friend or loved one, discuss the craft you are called to and your experiment in personalizing the practice before the practice.

- Later still, turn your experiment with the practice before the practice into a poem or story.

Going with the Stream

Never give up, then surrender.
YOGANANDA

The paradox in Yogananda's quote is profound advice that is hard to follow. What finally opened me to this wisdom was watching fish struggle through rough river currents into the mouth of a delta that took them effortlessly into the sea. The end of their effort was to go with the stream. It's harder to accept this when the rough currents cause our suffering. Hard when in pain to imagine that something deep and quiet might carry us. But sometimes, we're asked to ride rough currents until some deeper sea of knowing can lift us. Though it's hard to make sense of it, holding on and letting go work hand in hand. This paradox also applies to the life of expression.

The painter Henri Matisse was constantly working to put himself in a position to see the essence of things clearly and then to surrender to what he managed to see. In 1912, Matisse visited Morocco to see firsthand the mysterious landscape he'd stumbled onto in the paintings of Eugène Delacroix. While there, he immersed himself in three new canvases prompted by the Villa Brooks estate near his hotel. He went home inspired. But as the months passed, he was afraid he'd missed the essence of the scene. So, a year later, he brought the second canvas, *Acanthus*, back to Morocco. He returned to the same spot and immersed himself again, finally deciding, after all that way, to make no change.

What are we to learn from this? That seeing and painting, like feeling and writing, like awareness and compassion, are seamless manifestations of effort and surrender. The effort to keep his rendering of the Moroccan landscape accurate, and his effort to return, and his effort to conclude, after all that way, that there was no more to be done—all this is as much a part of the process of painting as putting brush to canvas.

Matisse confirms for us that effort leads to surrender and that both lead to a greater form of seeing. And that greater instance of seeing in turn leads us to work harder at learning from what we've seen. Whether we consider ourselves artists or not, we are all involuntary artisans stuck in the effort of living, with its unpredictable openings of grace that carry us along and make us feel complete from time to time.

One of the braveries of perseverance is the commitment to *keep* looking, again and again, to *keep* returning to what moves us and intrigues us, as we might return to shy teachers who need to know that we're not giving up before they'll reveal their teachings.

Monet offers us another great example of Yogananda's wisdom. From 1892 to 1893, Monet rented an apartment across from the Rouen Cathedral in order to paint more than thirty views of the church façade in different light. Something in the play of light on that cathedral wouldn't let go of the Impressionist. Only by immersing himself could he get closer to what kept stirring him. Similarly, Matisse was fascinated with the visage of the Cathedral of Notre Dame in Paris. From 1894 to 1907, he rented an apartment so he could stay in conversation with its changing face. He said, "I never tire of it. For me, it is always new."

Regardless of what these great painters produced by way of their devotion, what is most instructive is the immeasurable way their *seeing* changed for staying so engaged and then surrendering. Sustained inquiry changes how we see and hear and *that* changes how we know life and the world. Like a climber who never gives up, we arrive at the summit, only to surrender to the vastness that transforms us.

I recently experienced my own version of never giving up, not knowing how I would be asked to surrender. About ten years ago, a poem came to me called "In Singing the Secrets." That poem ended with the line "In place of wings, God gave us love." It was clear, even then, that the poem had midwifed a line greater than the expression that carried it.

About six years later, I was shaping my collection of poems, *The Way Under the Way*, and included this poem. In revising the manuscript, I realized that the poem actually ended before that line. This led me to a standoff between never giving up and surrendering. If this had happened in my forties, and not in my sixties, I would have kept the line no matter what. But twenty years is sometimes enough to bridge us from never giving up to surrendering. And so, I cut the line and saved it, not knowing for what.

Now, let's move forward to last winter. I was looking around in a massive file that held 150 pages cut from my book *The One Life We're Given*, as well as sixty pages of notes toward a new book, and almost eighty pages cut from my book *More Together Than Alone*. I didn't cut the extra chapters from these books because of their merit. The chapters are fine. But like the poem, it became clear in finishing these books that their organic structure couldn't bear all that material.

At the time, I had only intended to get an overview of this massive bundle of notes and drafts. But as soon as I dove in, the book woke before me like a sleeping giant and said, "Now! You must tend to me Now!" I've learned not to ignore such graces. I put everything aside and began to retrieve the book into being.

In six numinous weeks, I had a complete draft of my book *The Temple Is the World*. All the work of noting and drafting, of finding and saving, of writing and cutting, of putting in and taking out, had led me to a place of surrender through which I received the book in its entirety. The only thing left was to write a culminating story to close the book. I looked over the entire manuscript like an explorer mapping his steps through a forest to the open field at the far end. When I reached the end of what I'd written, the final story came as easily as the book. And to my surprise, when I reached the end of the final chapter, it was clear that the line "In place of wings, God gave us love" was supposed to be the last line of this book.

I don't know how this works, but years ago the earlier poem had brought me the last line for the end of a book I hadn't yet met. I'm always amazed at this process, how one meaningful thing carries another. I could have easily lost the line or insisted that it end the earlier poem. And so, never giving up until we're drawn to surrender is central to the process of creativity and expression. The rewards are infinite when we keep looking.

Here's one more example that continues to inspire me. In 1915, in the early days of cinema, a two-minute black-and-white film was made in which Renoir in his seventies has a paintbrush taped to his right hand because of his severe arthritis. Wide-eyed, he stares like a young student at a canvas we never see, pokes the brush, looks closely at some model out of view, then pokes the brush at the canvas again. Then he turns to the camera, exuberant, almost giddy, astonished one more time at the bliss his effort leads him to.

Sustained inquiry changes how we see and hear,
and that changes how we know life and the world.

An Invitation to Follow Material Over Time

• In your journal, enter a process of discovery over
  a month's time, retrieving each week one image,
  story, or detail of life that touches you. Describe
  each image, story, or detail thoroughly unto itself.
  Put these four expressions away for another month.
  Then, return and weave these four expressions
  into one story or reflection. See what arises.

• Later, in conversation with a friend or loved
  one, tell the story of your discovery of the
  culminating piece that you wrote.

Everything We Need

On a recent trip to New York, my wife, Susan, and I wandered into St. Thomas Episcopal Church for the first time, looking for a spot of quiet in the city. Instantly, we fell into a hushed space. As our hearts grew accustomed to the stillness, we saw, at the far end of the church, behind the altar, something luminous and looming. It was *The Great Reredos*. The word *reredos* is Middle English for a screen or decoration behind an altar, a popular construction in churches throughout Europe in the fourteenth and fifteenth centuries.

That day, we stood before one of the largest altar screens in the world. It looms there like the opened and worn wall of an Ancestral Pueblo cliff in which sixty cave-like perches offer glimpses of life-size sculptures in scenes upon scenes of life unfolding. The sculptures depict everyone from Savonarola—the Dominican friar who was burned in the main square of Florence, Italy, in 1498—to Bishop Selwyn, who was the first Anglican Bishop of New Zealand in 1841. There are even niches for George Washington and the British Prime Minister William Gladstone.

But the massive wall, sculpted in relief, is even more powerful without knowing who is depicted. For each of us, in simple and lasting anonymity, lives on the wall of life. Peering out from the edge between light and dark, we all struggle to find meaning and peace while surviving the rough slap of the elements and the wear and weight of time. This is the fate of humanity: to weather the cost of standing in the open in order to be guided by the angels. Each of us must inhabit our own perch in the wall of life in order to survive and thrive. Withstanding the weather of the days, we peer into the vastness, listening for the larger voices to tell us how to live. No one is exempt from this process, and no one can do it alone.

Earlier, I mentioned that the nineteenth-century English poet Gerard Manley Hopkins called the perch we each inhabit our "inscape." He described this as the inner nature of a person that connects our soul with the world. However, Hopkins is a sad example of how denying the gifts you already have will keep you from what you need.

Hopkins was born with an expressive force within him. Yet in 1866, while studying at Oxford, he had an unexpected sense of restraint that overtook his life. He began to suppress his expressiveness and gave up poetry for Lent. By July, he converted to Catholicism and, resolving to be strictly religious, he gave up poetry and burned his poems, certain they were a distraction from his want to follow God. He became a Jesuit priest.

But the tension between his innate drive to express his inwardness and his ascetic vow to withdraw from life in order to be closer to God plagued Hopkins the rest of his life. This division of purpose never left him. And he never benefited from the generation of mystics and Romantics that came before him, who showed us that a lasting path to the Divine nature in all things is *through* the life of expression, not by avoiding it. His predecessors included William Blake, William Wordsworth, Samuel Taylor Coleridge, and Goethe.

Despite his ascetic commitment, Hopkins couldn't suppress the force of his heartfelt imagination. His sense of inscape was ever present, even when describing a dead tree. This is from his journals:

> There is one notable dead tree . . . the inscape
> markedly holding its most simple and beautiful
> oneness up from the ground through a graceful
> swerve below [to] the spring of the branches up to
> the tops of the timber. I saw the inscape freshly, as if
> my mind were still growing. . . .

Still, he kept himself from writing poems for seven years. Until five nuns drowned in a shipwreck, and his abbot asked him to write a poem to help put their souls to rest. And so, at the age of thirty-one, Hopkins wrote "The Wreck of the *Deutschland*." Though he never felt in complete integrity, he kept writing for the rest of his life. This tension led to long bouts of depression and religious doubt.

In 1877, he wrote "The Caged Skylark," an obvious image of the inner strain he felt, and also wrote "The Windhover" with the lines, "My heart in hiding stirred for a bird." Staying devout to Catholicism, he refused to publish any of his poems. He died of typhoid fever in 1879 at the age of forty-four.

In complete contrast to the restraint Hopkins endured, we can look to Beethoven's incredible fortitude in composing unprecedented music in spite of going deaf. He was unfailing in expressing what came through him, whether he could hear it played or not.

Listening to a performance of Beethoven's String Quartet no. 14, opus 131, Franz Schubert, a contemporary, remarked, "After this, what is left for us to write?" Completed in 1826, opus 131 was considered groundbreaking, offering seven emotionally rising movements instead of the traditional four—all played without pause. Beethoven's compositions for string quartet rush players into dynamic and intimate relationship with the music, the way the river of experience rushes us into dynamic and intimate relationship with life.

This is the inspiring lesson of Beethoven's opus 131: it mirrors the nonstop demand of life to have us make music of what we're given, not knowing what will happen next. Inevitably, having to play seven movements without pause, the instruments will go out of tune. With no time to re-tune the strings, the musicians have to adjust and improvise within the structure of the music.

In this piece, Beethoven insists on allowing both the harmony and discord of life to be present. He challenges the musicians to see the movements through, even out of tune.

In just this way, we are challenged every day to say yes to the movements of life, seeing them through, without pause, staying in relationship to the music of life and each other, adjusting as we go, not knowing what will happen next. Yet even out of tune, this messy and magnificent practice, so essentially human, will let us hear—briefly—the music of the Universe being the Universe. The moments of hearing this larger music while grinding out the smaller music of our lives is what sages of all traditions have called glimpses of Eternity.

So, though there are times to rest and times to rehearse, the blessings and resources of life rush into the flawed and raw openings that mark our inscape when we keep playing without pause, reaching for ways to find the unknown harmonies between us. It's as if, for all his brilliance of composition, Beethoven's strength of heart confirmed through his creations that a moment of meeting life completely is more rewarding than an ounce of refinement. It's inspiring and helpful to realize that saying yes when we feel depleted and out of tune wakes the sleeping genie of our soul who smiles to say, when looking at our trouble, "I've been waiting for this. You have everything you need."

The truth is we have both the reluctance of Hopkins and the fortitude of Beethoven deep within us, never knowing which will surface. Which is why we need each other—to surface our inscape in the world rather than suppress it.

With this in mind, consider that "to rehearse" means to repeat aloud, to come alive, and to rake our way against death. This implies that repeating what we know to be true can put off death for the moment and bring us alive. And so, every time we sing, dance, or speak the truth, we rehearse what it means to be alive and keep death at arm's length for a while. This is at the heart of any creative endeavor, be it song, dance, theater, or the confession of our love.

More than two hundred years after Hopkins and Beethoven, another lesson, almost lost, surfaced in the ruins of Europe. Several months after World War II had ended, Fabian von Schlabrendorff returned to what was left of his home in Pätzig, Germany, and found nothing intact. Fabian was a friend of Dietrich Bonhoeffer, the Lutheran pastor who was hung for his part in a failed assassination attempt on Hitler. Fabian shuffled through the rubble of his home, missing his friends, missing his wife, missing his life before the war.

He overturned remnants in what was his kitchen, but whatever was useable had been stolen. As he searched through what was his library, only one item lay undamaged among the broken shelves. It was Bonhoeffer's book, *Emulating the Way of the Master*, whose English title is *The Cost of Discipleship*. Eerily, that was all that was left. The sad German sat on the pile of torn and broken books that had spilled their voices into the ashes. He sat there on his ruined perch and opened his dead friend's book.

It is telling that this small volume is all that survived, telling that Bonhoeffer's title in German doesn't signify a particular master but refers to the master within that carries us, the master of being that we follow with our heart and soul. It is revealing that the English title misses the point, only seeing the cost of following our heart and soul in the world. From inside, following what we know to be true is a devotion of infinite reward. From outside, giving of ourselves so deeply is only measured in terms of cost.

This is equally true for artists and writers, or anyone trying to live an authentic life. If we only see the hard, uncertain work before us in terms of its cost in the world, we will be thwarted before we begin. But if we can discover our way of expression by emulating the rhythm of our being, the way a bird emulates the wind, we will be carried as easily as a bird in glide.

Each of the previous stories is an example of a soul looking out from their perch in the wall of life. From Hopkins, we learn not to deny or suppress our gifts. From Beethoven, we learn to be steadfast with our heart, tuning as we go. And from Bonhoeffer, we learn to emulate the way of being in our soul, despite the cost of being who we are in the world.

No matter our call or plight, these lessons are covenants of the life of expression, available to each of us as we peer out from the wall of life. Ultimately, we can trust that when facing what we're given and tuning as we go, we will have everything we need.

Each of us must inhabit our own perch in the wall of life in order to survive and thrive. Withstanding the weather of the days, we peer into the vastness, listening for the larger voices to tell us how to live.

An Invitation to Tune as You Go

- In your journal, describe a time when you suppressed your own voice. What caused you to do this? How did this affect you? Later, create a poem or story about someone struggling with an inner tension that suppresses their own voice.

- In conversation with a friend or loved one, tell the story of a time when you were compelled to tune as you go. Later, create a poem or story about someone having to tune as they go.

- Now, apply what you're learning from your journaling and conversation to some creative endeavor that is currently calling you. What is this creative pull asking of you?

Part 4

Becoming One With

No matter the press and hurry of the world, what matters comes slowly. And slipping through the noise in our souls and the chaos in the world, we can spend more time on the inside of things. The longer we practice being present and letting what we experience move through us, the closer we come to becoming the poem.

For being here without looking away leads us into the magic of liberty. And letting life play its song of a thousand moods through our heart leads us into the timeless river. When faithful to a life of expression, we can discover the moment of being that belongs to everyone, and know whatever moment we are in is home.

The final part of this book examines the rhythms of wakefulness and sensitivity that open before us as we get closer and closer to life. Whether you are an artist or not, the hope, the goal, is to become one with all we encounter through our enlivened practice of expression.

The Magic of Liberty

Art brings us into close contact with the mysterious goodness at the core of what it means to be human.

HENK BRANDT

Slipping Through

When I was starting out, I wanted so badly to become a poet that I held it in view like some hill I needed to climb to see from. But getting to the top, something was missing, and so I had to climb the next hill. Finally, I realized I didn't need to climb to become a poet, I was a poet.

The same thing happened with love. I wanted so badly to love and be loved, but climbing through relationships like hills, I realized again that I was loving and loved all along.

Then I wanted to become wise, but after much travel and study, it was during my bedridden days with cancer that I realized I was already wise. I just didn't know the language of my wisdom.

Now I understand that all these incarnations come alive in us when we dare to live the days before us—when we dare to listen to the wind singing in our veins. We carry the love and wisdom like seeds, and the days sprout us. And it's the sprouting that's the poetry. It's the sprouting that's the long road to freedom.

Another lesson is more recent. It comes from a conversation I had with a very wise woman who was a mentor to me. I mentioned her earlier. She was the Jungian analyst Helen Luke. I knew Helen during the last two years of her life, and during what turned out to be our last conversation, she said to me, "Yours is to live it, not to reveal it." This troubled me, for I have spent my life becoming a writer, thinking that my job has been just that—to reveal what is essential and hidden.

In the time since Helen died, I've come to understand her last instruction as an invitation to shed any grand purpose, no matter how devoted we may be to what we are doing. She wasn't telling me to stop writing, but to stop striving to be important. She was inviting me to stop *recording* the poetry of life and to *enter* the poetry of life.

This applies to us all. If we devote ourselves to the life at hand, the rest will follow. For life, it seems, reveals itself through those willing to live. Anything else, no matter how beautiful, is just advertising.

This took me many years to learn and accept. Having begun innocently enough there arose separations, and now I know that health resides in restoring direct experience. Thus, having struggled to do what has never been done, I discovered that living is the original art.

Let me say all this another way. When I began, the goal was to find the stream of creativity so I might drink from it and net the poems and books rushing by. But after almost dying from cancer in my thirties, it became clear that there is no stream to search out and find. The waters of life are all around us. We are forever in it and cannot separate ourselves from it.

By my late forties, all the nets I'd woven over a lifetime had worn through, and the moments worth rendering as poems and stories and books kept slipping through. Still, I caught what I could. At first this was maddening, then ironic and ultimately laughable and perfect: a metaphor itself for the humble spark we are, trying so hard to light everything when, if blessed, it is we who are ignited by our friction with the world.

Now in my sixties, a new art presents itself, which is the oldest art of all: *letting* the fishlike truths *slip on through*. Now there is nothing to net. Now the cut-open nets themselves, with their tracings and silhouettes of what passes through—these are the writings I dry, decipher, and share.

Just the other day, I traced this small poem:

After all my hunger and failed attempts,
I wake like a fisherman waist-high in a
stream of salmon tearing through my
nets; pulling me along to the waters
of our birth.

In my dreams, I imagine that the ancient cave paintings of
fish are not sketches on stone but the rubbings of some early
fishermen who having lost their catch pressed their empty net
to the cave wall in order to save some trace of the life that
slipped through.

Having struggled to do what has never been done,
I discovered that living is the original art.

An Invitation to Know Your Own Wisdom

- In your journal, describe something dear that slipped
  through your net and what it means to you.

- In conversation with a friend or loved
  one, describe an experience that revealed to
  you an aspect of your own wisdom.

Living in the Gap

It is the writer's privilege to help one
endure by lifting up his heart.
WILLIAM FAULKNER

When I was thirty, I traveled to London for the first time to visit a friend in grad school. I immediately felt the history in the old buildings and streets. My second day there, we took the Underground from Victoria Station. As our train arrived, I realized that the space between the platform and the train was much greater than in the States. I looked at the edge of the platform. And there, etched in the concrete, was the phrase, "Mind the Gap." The phrase instantly seemed an instruction from the gods.

Mind the gap between stillness and motion. Mind the gap between who we are and who we hope to be. Mind the gap between what's visible and what's not. Mind the gap between the inner life and the outer life. The phrase has stayed with me ever since—for our search for meaning depends on how we mind the gap and how we enter the spaces between things. While a tree is all leaves, the life of the tree is in the spaces filled with wind between the leaves. And while we are the sum of our actions and words, the life of who we are is in the spaces filled with Spirit between our actions and words.

In time, minding the gap leads to entering the gap, which leads to living in the spaces between what is known and what remains unknown. The gap between the details of the world is where we find the invisible energy that holds everything together. And so, one of the challenges for the writer in us is to pin down the physical details in life so the invisible can show through the spaces between them—the way a window frames a view, the way a door frames a threshold, the way painting everything that is not the path makes the path visible.

Throughout time, people have argued whether the world is only what we see or if the physical world is the manifestation of the essence of life, the way the tip of an iceberg is only what's visible of an enormous foundation that remains out of view. Trusting that there is an Invisible Whole that brings the world into view has led to more intuitive forms of art.

In the 1930s, Surrealism was burgeoning worldwide as a means to explore the Hidden Wholeness that informs the world as we know it. Realizing that the artist's intention was no longer the aim, painters began to experiment with techniques that would evoke paintings beyond their control. Whatever an artist could imagine was only a catalyst enlisted to release a creative force that couldn't be foreseen.

One innovative technique was decalcomania, which, though first used in the 1700s to transfer images to pottery, was used by Surrealists to apply a wet medium, such as ink or gouache, to a sheet of paper that is then pressed against another sheet of paper. When pulled apart, unexpected patterns appear on the second sheet of paper, beyond the artist's intention or control.

This process of image discovery offers a useful way to understand what happens to us when our intentions meet reality. In truth, it's very rare that what we intend ever manifests exactly in the world. We often mistake the gap between what we intend and what happens as a form of failure or falling short. In actuality, it's what we discover in the gap that causes us to grow. For the press of our intentions against reality reveals unexpected patterns that hold life's secrets. What we view as spillage often holds the gold.

We waste too much time trying to make our intentions come true, rather than entering the unseen field that waits beyond our intentions. We waste too much energy trying to make reality mirror our dreams. The real work of experience resides in reading the unexpected patterns that the press of life reveals, finding direction and meaning there. Try as we do to resist what we're given, the press of what we want against what we're given is the way we discover the patterns of truth.

In the 1940s, the German photographer Lotte Jacobi kept exploring the spaces between things by moving torches and candles over light-sensitive paper and capturing the unexpected patterns that would emerge. These artistic explorations frame the creative act as a conversation with the unknown rather than the imprint of our will in shaping materials. Mind the Gap!

On my return from that first trip to London, I became a student of the gap between what we intend and what we discover. Over the years, I stopped visiting the spaces between things and started living there. That is, I started meeting the world from the inside of life rather than darting from one external circumstance to another. What I've learned from this is that the heart is the perceptual organ that braids the unseeable with the seeable. The heart is the instrument that connects us to the enormous foundation that remains out of view. And so, by minding the gap and living in the gap, we help each other endure, as William Faulkner says, by lifting each other's heart.

We enter this process of connection and endurance by being faithful to the details around us, giving them our wholehearted attention until they point to the life-force between them, the way two strokes in a Sumi painting compel us to enter the charged space between them.

By its very nature, what lives underneath the physical world is hard to name. Trying to point to all that matters led me to this poem, which, like all poems, points to the spaces between the words:

Wordless Dancer

There is a dancer who sways beneath
all I know. She can't be summoned,
only followed. I have been her apprentice for years. She has led me to you
and to poetry and to the soft truth
inside suffering. If pressed, I'd say
she shimmers before I sing and
thunders when I cry. She turns
every why into how and calms my
doubts the way water smoothes each
hole in sand. Oh she won't come out
while we're talking like this, but
only when we drop our words
and put down everything
we don't want to put down.

*One of the challenges for the writer in us is to pin
down the physical details in life so the invisible
can show through the spaces between them.*

An Invitation to Enter
the Spaces in Between

- Take a walk and find a place to sit for a while. Then, as a painter might sketch the details of the scene, describe in your journal the details before you as carefully as you can. Then, enter the gap between the details and record what you sense is there holding the details together.

- In conversation with a friend or loved one, discuss what the phrase "Mind the Gap" means to you.

Becoming the Poem

Over the years, I have found that the life of expression has helped to thin what stands between me and life. This is one of the purposes of creativity. The life of expression has, in fact, helped me enter life more than watch it. Poetry has always been a way to point to pockets of life-force that bring us alive and keep us together. To become the poem means that we, ourselves, become the carriers of life-force that hold the world together.

A great example of this comes from the life of the German philosopher Friedrich Nietzsche. The story goes that on January 3, 1889, he was approached by two policemen after making some sort of public disturbance in the streets of Turin, Italy. It seems he saw a horse being whipped at the other end of the Piazza Carlo Alberto, and in that moment, there was nothing between him and the pain of the horse being whipped. And so he ran to the horse, throwing his arms around its neck to protect it. Then he collapsed. He never recovered. Some regard this event as embarrassing, and yet it just might be Nietzsche's crowning moment of integrity on par with St. Francis of Assisi displaying his unmitigated love for all of God's creatures.

I find it beautiful and heartbreaking that all the vast and tenacious thinking of such a prodigious mind should undo itself—quite naturally and poignantly—into the compassionate act of protecting a horse from being whipped. All his deep thinking led him, in that moment, to stand between the whip and the whipped. Isn't this the aim of all writing, of all art? When we can say yes and throw our arms around the hurt one's neck, then what feels necessary stuns us with its splendor. For all Nietzsche wrote, that one fully lived moment was the poem of his life.

Who knows what this moment is for each of us and when it will appear? Yet I believe that the practice of integrity, the practice of love and truth, and the commitment to a life of expression, whatever its form, help ready us for this moment of becoming the poem.

Inevitably, life is a journey of moving in and out of the light, of falling off course and steering our way back to center. If this is so, then freezing a moment of being on course and calling that success, and freezing a moment of falling off course and calling that failure are useless distinctions. Neither helps us to see or engage the practice of being awake in the stream of life. Once discovering that we are constantly in process, that we are constantly unfolding, the goal is not to solidify our character and views, but to stay devoted to how we—and what we think and feel—evolve.

The purpose of memoir and autobiographical writing, then, is not to chronicle ourselves as the star of our own movie, but to inquire into our changing experience deeply enough and honestly enough that we touch on the common experience of all life. The way a biologist can reveal the dynamics of life by looking at one cell, we can reveal the depths of the human journey by steadfastly rooting our story in the particulars of our own unfolding, looking for where those particulars join with other life. As looking thoroughly at one cell reveals the nature of all cells, looking thoroughly at the heart of our story reveals the nature of all stories.

One reward for aligning our life with other life is that we are then allowed to draw on the strength of what we have in common with all life. When you look at a mountain from a distance, it stands up from the horizon, singular and rugged.

But closer up, it's impossible to tell where the mountain stops and the earth begins. What makes the mountain so steadfast and everlasting is that its core is resting on the foundational core of the earth. Indeed, the very center of the mountain is aligned with the very center of the earth. This makes the mountain strong beyond its own constitution.

In just this way, when we can stand by our core, we're not just standing on our own constitution but aligning our center with the Center of All Life. In such moments, it's hard to tell where the individual soul stops and the foundation of all Spirit begins. This alignment opens us to strength beyond our own. By being thoroughly ourselves, we stand on what can last and gain access to all the resources of life. In actuality, the courage to stand by our core until we can align with the core of everything is the beginning of resilience. And the practice of writing, or any other form of expression, helps us to be thoroughly ourselves. Such a practice enables us to stand by our core and to align our center with the Center of All Life.

Until tumbling on the other side of cancer, I never would have imagined that surviving and creating were so close. In fact, in the heat of living, they are identical. In our deepest moments of living, when life writes us, it is the poetic quality of healing that matters, no matter the form of art or truth that carries it. In our complete and honest moments of expression, surviving is entering life and creating as we go, and healing is the moment when the Center of All Life moves through our center as we stand between the whip and the whipped.

As looking thoroughly at one cell reveals the nature
of all cells, looking thoroughly at the heart of
our story reveals the nature of all stories.

An Invitation to Be a Conduit

- In your journal, describe a time when you were a
  brief conduit between other living things. What
  did such a moment offer to those around you, and
  how did such a moment affect you? Later, write
  a poem or story about someone who becomes a
  brief conduit between other living things.

- In conversation with a friend or loved one, discuss
  what the phrase "Becoming the Poem" means to you.

- Go for a ride or walk and arrive at a place—in a
  café, in the woods, or in your backyard—where you
  can be still enough to receive other life. Let other
  life enter you and leave you. Let life flow through
  you, and note what it says to you as it moves
  through. Then, journal the story of this experience.

The Empty Saddle

The artist has the right to make one thing out of
many and a world out of the smallest part.
RAINER MARIA RILKE

What we discover and uncover stays with us, and then we are called to stay true to what touches us. But how? By honoring the fact that, though we all need to be seen and heard, what we see is more important than being seen. Though he was legendary in his own time, the sculptor Auguste Rodin suffered harsh rejection because of the boldness of his work. Still, he remained loyal and steadfast to the clay and marble that spoke to him. Rilke described Rodin's love of process this way:

> His work alone spoke to him. It spoke to him in
> the morning when he awoke, and in the evening it
> reverberated in his hands long after he had laid it aside,
> like music in an instrument one has ceased to play.

I recognize the deep effect of what we are led to. I am often reverberating with images at night that I have wrestled into view during the day. They linger on my hands as I try to understand what meaning they carry.

One such image came to me in a very short story about a cyclist who has trained for months to compete in a race. On the day of the race, he is so far ahead that he can barely see the other racers. As he glides down the far side of a hill, a great blue heron suddenly appears, wings fully spread, above his handlebars. He is stunned and stops, straddling the bike. The story moves years ahead, when the cyclist is asked, "What cost you the race?" He stares out into the woods behind his home and says, "I didn't lose the race. I left it."

The image of the heron instantly became my guide. I started to read about herons and began to watch herons. I even tried to draw them. In time, the book the story was a part of, *As Far As the Heart Can See*, was accepted for publication. I put the story about the cyclist and the heron as the first piece in the book. But when my editor gave me her first round of edits, she wanted me to cut the heron from the story. I was dumbfounded.

This revealed such a chasm between us that I realized we had a very different understanding of life and no common language. Hard as it was, I pulled the book from the publisher. I was heartbroken and somewhat lost. In other instances, it would have been easy to change the story or substitute another image. But I couldn't move forward in this case, because asking me to cut the heron from the story was asking me to abandon what I saw in order to be seen. And this is at the crux of being who we are. It took three more years to find another publisher who marveled at the appearance of the heron as I did.

In writing each book since, I've been transformed by their creation into a conduit of love and an agent of care, which I now believe is how creating and expressing shape us. This understanding led to the following poem:

A Thirst for Simple Light

At first, it's about achieving.
Creating something that might last.
Then having the thing so carefully

carried break before our eyes. And
building it again. Only to have our
foundation crack. If we have the strength,
we might keep building. But sooner or later,
we turn to help others carry simple things
or find what's been lost. And one day,
purpose is a fugitive who's forgotten
why he's on the run. And as the body
is worn to only what matters, we are
worn to care, not build. To Care.
About anything. About whatever is
before us. Singing. Packing groceries.
Learning the names of all the leaves
on Earth. Collecting movies that have
life in the title and giving them away.
Anything that keeps us tumbling like
bottles of light destined to break
for those thirsty enough to
drop their need of cups.

None of this is new. It's just our turn to discover the grace of what it means to be here. One of my favorite images comes from Basho. In 1689, he was walking around the island of Japan and didn't know the way. He asked a farmer who said, "It's easier if you just take my horse. He knows the way. When you get to the next town, just let him go and he'll come home." So Basho was led by this majestic creature and, once in the next town, he tied a gift to the empty saddle and sent the horse home.

That image of the riderless horse with a gift tied to its empty saddle touches me. Perhaps because I've been lost so many times over the years. Perhaps because I've been quietly saved by the kindness of strangers. Perhaps because some of my most satisfying moments as a human being have risen from the anonymous giving that we are sometimes called to offer. Perhaps because being a spirit in the world is so much like following a riderless horse that we lose and share and return to each other.

The images of the heron and the empty saddle have been great teachers. And following the heron and tying a gift to the empty saddle is now the work I'm devoted to.

In writing each book, I've been transformed by their creation into a conduit of love and an agent of care, which I now believe is how creating and expressing shape us.

An Invitation to Follow
What Speaks and to Give

- In your journal, describe a part of the natural world that has become a totem for you. In my case, it was a heron. It might be a turtle or a willow or a broken shell from the sea. Research the history of your totem and explore how all this is speaking to you.

- When you can, tie a gift to the empty saddle of someone who has helped you on your way. In conversation with a friend or loved one, tell your story of tying a gift to the empty saddle. Later, write a poem or story about the empty saddle.

The Timeless River

*It's a process of approaching the unwritten and
the unspoken and the unspeakable. And the closer
you get to it, the more life there seems to be.*
ARTHUR MILLER

Feeling is the only sense we have.
KURTIS LAMKIN

*In writing poetry, I listen
and look for ways to throw
paint on the invisible.*
DEANNA NIKAIDO

What Matters Comes Slowly

It does not do to hurry.
AUGUSTE RODIN

Poems come slowly. They break surface like dolphins after long stretches of going under. So writing a book of poems for me is different than writing my other books. With poems, I have to sit when I'm able and try to make heart-sense of what life has been doing to me and with me. Like wringing out a sponge, I squeeze what matters onto the page, let it dry, and see what's there the next day. One by one, they gather into an instructive whole. All this to say that in trying to make sense of my own experience, I discovered a theme to the journey—that over the years we are all worn away of excess and made elemental. To survive this process, we often need to hold each other up in order to discover and return to what matters.

William Carlos Williams wrote, "It is difficult to get the news from poems yet men die miserably every day for lack of what is found there." We run from crisis to crisis, looking for our worth in all the wrong places, wanting to be loved and honored, when suffering only humbles us to the eternal task of loving and honoring. Why? Because things that matter take time, so we might outwait all urgency and outgrow our ambitions. Then, with nowhere to go, we are forced to accept ourselves, as we are, and care for everything and everyone from the bare moment we wake in.

In one of his last poems, called "my prayer," E. E. Cummings said, "God make me the poet of simplicity, force, and clearness." These are qualities that we can only settle into. And so, the life of expression is made for the long haul, a marriage between heart and soul wherever life takes us.

The French poet and screenwriter Jacques Prévert, who survived the insanity of World War II, speaks carefully about the patience deep expression takes in this poem written in the 1940s:

To Paint the Portrait of a Bird

Paint first a cage
with an open door
paint then
something pretty
something simple
something handsome
something useful
for the bird
then place the canvas against a tree
in a garden
in a wood
or in a forest
hide behind the tree
silently
motionless
Sometimes the bird arrives at once
but it may also take many years
before making up its mind
Do not be discouraged
wait
wait if need be many years
a speedy or a delayed arrival
bears no relation

to the success of the portrait
When the bird arrives
if it arrives
observe the most profound silence
wait until the bird enters the cage
and when it has entered
close the door gently with a stroke of the brush
then
paint out one by one all the bars of the cage
taking care to touch none of the bird's feathers
Paint then the portrait of a tree
choosing the loveliest of its branches
for the bird
paint too the green foliage and the fresh wind
the dust of the sun
and the noise of insects
in the grass in the summer heat
and then wait for the bird to sing
If the bird does not sing
it is a bad sign
a sign that the picture is bad
but if it sings it is a good sign
a sign that you can sign
So you pluck gently then
one of the bird's feathers
and you write your name
in a corner of the portrait.

The two great lessons from this poem are: "Wait, wait if need be many years, a speedy or a delayed arrival bears no relation to the success of the portrait," and "Wait for the bird to sing. If the bird does not sing, it is a bad sign, a sign that the picture is bad." How long things take to reveal themselves is no measure of our worth. And even after years of work, if the work doesn't sing, we need to start over. These are simple but hard truths to face.

Yet in spite of the difficulties we face in receiving what comes to us, the river of the deep never stops flowing through us. The Chinese poet Su Tung-P'o of the Song Dynasty said, "How many thousands of poems have flowed through me tonight! And tomorrow I won't be able to repeat even one word."

So, when not doing well, when full of doubt or pain or worry, when unable to find your way, try, very slowly, to return to moments that feel foundational. By "foundational" I mean moments that are solid, in which you feel directly connected to life, in which you feel safe and thorough, in which you feel at peace, even for a few seconds.

You don't have to name these foundational moments, or explain them, or fit them into some theological box. You simply have to experience them and locate them, so you have a chance to return to them or to moments like them, when you need to.

In time, you will chart a constellation of foundational moments that can hold you up when you fall down. And mysteriously, when identified and honored, these moments of peace and clearness start to join. So, in time, our foundational field enlarges when we have the courage to find and receive what will hold us up.

Such a moment might be watching the apple blossoms fold over in the wind. Or falling into the rhythm of chopping vegetables in the afternoon light. Or watching the runoff in spring rush around a fallen limb. You'll know these moments are foundational when you can't reduce them or be distracted from them. Such a moment might be listening to your ninety-year-old mother breathe while she sleeps. Or watching a young woman well up on her cell phone, not sure what she is hearing, but knowing that you are watching a life living.

Despite our want to speed things up and pin things down, we're called to move slowly as a way to inhabit life more than name it. The greatest way we can practice this is by staying in conversation with the Mystery of Life itself. It's more important to experience the Unnamed Mystery as it moves through us and about us than to argue if that enormous presence is God, Nature, Physics, or the Bareness of Being that Buddhists speak of. Ultimately, names are only useful as doorways to what can't be named. Like a gymnast tumbling steadfast through the air, patience is the strength of soul that lets us glide ever so slowly through the eye of the Universe.

How long things take to reveal themselves is no measure of our worth. And even after years of work, if the work doesn't sing, we need to start over. These are simple but hard truths to face.

An Invitation to Learn from Patience

- In your journal, enter an experiment in patience by writing a line or sentence every other day, living life in between. Do this for two weeks and see what expression has revealed itself to you. Then shape that expression.

- In conversation with a friend or loved one, share the piece that you've retrieved through your experiment in patience and discuss the process.

The Table Between
Presence and Meaning

If I could tell you what it meant,
there would be no point in dancing it.
ISADORA DUNCAN

There is a table between presence and meaning before which we open our heart, trying to make sense of things. We each need such a table to see from and work at, so we can let in all that is. For writers, this worktable is set up on the edge of the world, where we peer authentically in all directions, trying to understand what it means to be alive.

For me, this begins every day at my desk, when I stare into the world of presence that waits beyond the window of the blank page. Then, I look out my study window into the outer world with its tangled majesty, with its thousand connections and disconnections that thread the changing tapestry of life. Like all those before me, I give of myself in both directions, letting the inner and outer world merge within me until presence and meaning stir me to explore something on the page, something the words try to point to, something I can voice with full integrity.

What, then, is your table, the one you work at, from which you look into our original presence and from which you look into life constantly unfolding? How do you let the voices of the soul and the voices of the world speak to each other through you? The blank page is the ordinary anvil a writer works at as a wordsmith forging tools and totems fit for the gods but left on the trail for others to find.

Pablo Neruda had his desk face the sea in his beloved home on Isla Negra, near Santiago, on the Chilean coast. And Thomas Merton had his sparse desk facing an open meadow at the Abbey of Gethsemani in Kentucky. But the Japanese poet Basho took his desk with him, as he walked around the island of Japan in 1689, noting his journey in a new hybrid of haiku and prose that he called a *haibun*.

Whether our table is actual or an inner place from which to look in all directions, being still at the juncture between presence and meaning opens the meditative space under all our masks and facades. This is where the practice of writing always turns real.

All the meditative traditions encourage us to be still and to drop our thoughts and feelings, so we can breathe our way below all trouble into the flow of life-force that carries us. This is wise counsel. It gives us perspective and sometimes peace. But being a poet, I enter that Universal space and just take notes. I lean into the stillness with an open heart and listen to everything, including my thoughts and feelings and the entanglements of life. For I believe the mutual goal of meditation and poetry is not to have us remove ourselves from the human journey, but to have us live our lives more completely in relationship to the flow of life-force that carries us.

The poems and all that I write are simply the trail and record of what I see and feel in the meditative space. All my writings arise from peering from the edge of our humanness into the bareness of being that permeates all life. I have intuitively worked this way, even as a boy, long before I knew about meditation or poetry. I believe that poetry itself resides at the holy juncture where our humanness touches the bareness of being that holds the Universe together. This is the only place I write from, whether I'm alone in the woods or being jostled on a crowded subway. It is the lens through which I meet life. It is the place I return to in order to renew this endless conversation. It is listening in this space that keeps me fresh and sane.

When I can be still and honor this deep meditative space, life shows up. My dear friend, the great visionary educator Parker Palmer, speaks of the soul as a force of life at home in the wild terrains of our heart. In this, the soul is so elemental that it is both indispensable and untamable. Parker says that we often stomp around like loud campers in the forest, harping for the soul and other forces of life to come out of hiding, while we scare them away. How stymied we are when they don't show their faces. Yet when I can quiet my fear and want and be as still as nature, the living aspects of the Universe will come out of the brush and even nuzzle beside me. So, at once, stillness brings us in alignment with our true nature, while allowing all forms of life to touch us.

Once in a while, the notion of a book appears. It's not that I make it up. It's not my idea. Rather, I come upon its possibility, the way a lifelong hiker comes upon a new trail. The trail has always been there. It's just that no one has walked it yet. For example, I was in Charleston, South Carolina, teaching at the Sophia Institute, a wonderful retreat center that I return to every year. I was in a wide-ranging conversation with my dear friend Henk Brandt. The magnolias were beginning to bloom, and the light was streaming over Henk's shoulder. Something in our conversation merged with the light on the magnolia, and I was stunned again that such blossoms should grow out of wood. Back in our conversation, Henk was talking about mitochondria and how they are key receptors lining every cell in our body. I was listening for the relevant metaphor in all this, as I always do.

It was then that I had a glimpse of a trail I hadn't seen before, and I met a book I've yet to write, called *Life Teachers:*

Metaphors from the Living Universe. Instantly, its landscape and structure appeared to me. What if I were to concentrate on using metaphor—the way an astrophysicist might use a telescope and a microbiologist might use a microscope—to understand the latticework of connections that make up life, both large and small? My mind had glimpsed all this in an instant, and I asked Henk to pause so I could jot down a schematic of what I'd glimpsed.

Later, I created a folder for the new book, setting up files for notes, fragments, quotes, and research. It is now in my life. This book will now be a port of inquiry that I will follow to its conclusion, probably for years. This is all we can do: wander through life earnestly on the look for trails we've yet to take, trails we're called to walk and name. Whatever our form of expression, we are best served when we can enter the unknown as a port of inquiry, mapping our way with our fragile yet resilient humanity.

Like a meteor hurtling toward Earth, each of us hurtles through the years being worn of all that doesn't matter. Like a meteor that shines brighter the more it casts off, each soul shines brighter as the body that carries it is slowly cast off over a lifetime. This is the same process our deepest feelings and understandings are subject to as we try to express them. Each truth shines brighter as the story that carries it is cast off in the telling and there is nothing left but its truth. And both the light of truth we carry in our story and the light of soul we carry in our lifetime illuminate us from the inside until we glow. Until someone sees the light in our eyes and is stopped by the force of life we carry and release by living.

All my writings arise from peering from the edge of our humanness into the bareness of being that permeates all life.

An Invitation to Relate to the Unknown

- In your journal, describe your favorite spot from which to write. Whether an actual table or an inner one, describe what you do to arrive at your table between presence and meaning.

- In conversation with a friend or loved one, discuss your relationship with the blank page.

Peering from the Edge

It's unclear exactly where and when John Keats carved out his famous poem "Ode on a Grecian Urn," but we do know that he was twenty-four and seriously ill, dying of consumption, what later would be known as tuberculosis. In a weakened state, he sailed for Rome in September of 1820. There, he would quickly wither away in an apartment perched halfway up the Spanish Steps. From his window, he had a slightly elevated view of the ancient city, a view comparable to the one he had climbed to in his short, precocious life. He had apprenticed to an apothecary and then qualified as a surgeon before being swept up by literature. But here, he knew that his trip to Rome, which had started as a hopeful convalescence, had turned into a private form of hospice.

Even before moving to Rome, we can see from his letters that he was growing, deepening, and widening quickly, and his tumble into suffering had only ripped him open further. He was in the midst of his own awakening and, as such, viewed his poetry to this point as adolescent. He was pained that he would not have the time to write from his newly excavated depth.

This is the context from which we can understand the crisis he couldn't escape. And from his courage in facing both life and death, from his courage not to look away, came one of the most profound insights in Western literature. Imagine a sorely awakened young man, dying of tuberculosis, watching the world go on. From this sore perch, he began "Ode on a Grecian Urn." For much of the poem, poor young Keats was lamenting his lack of time, crying inwardly for a way out. Though life and death had scoured him open to this deeper place, they both seemed harsh. If he could only stop the wheel of life and somehow get off. In his pain, he fantasized, understandably, that it would be easier to be a fixed figure on an ancient urn, frozen there but safe from the puncture and breakage of time.

The poem becomes a trail of someone who, in facing death, stumbles into a moment of profound perception opened by his suffering. It is further proof that the journey of honest expression leads to truth and even wisdom. His life was being snuffed, a day at a time, and while voicing his pain and complaints, it seems he suddenly tripped into deeper territory, as if he had come upon something vast and remarkable. Those last two lines of the poem are his exclamation at having seen this vastness: "Beauty is truth, truth beauty—that is all ye know on earth, and all ye need to know."

If not for those two last lines, we would never know this poem. Not only is Keats a poignant example of courage in facing crisis, his insight helps us to navigate life with grace. In revealing Truth and Beauty as the spiritual elements necessary to survive life, as necessary as air and water, he also reveals something important about their relationship. When he says, "Beauty is truth, truth beauty," the two are not identical. They are not interchangeable like A = B and B = A. For the way that Truth is beautiful is very different than the way that Beauty is truthful. Yet together, they are all the food we need to get by.

Beauty renews our vital connection to the Whole. It is full of awe and wonder. It renews our membership in all that is larger than us and makes the eternal perspective visible, though often briefly. In this, Beauty is always true. Truth, on the other hand, has a raw beauty all its own that arises from its stark, irreducible being. Truth, as a window into things as they are, is often difficult to receive. But truth is necessary to bring us to the edge of transformation, for it forces us to accept the brokenness in our humanness and in the world. From here, we can begin to rearrange and repair. No one would say that the

Holocaust was beautiful. But the truth of that awful time has its own irrevocable starkness, which must be faced and never forgotten, if we are to keep compassion alive.

So Keats, in peering from the edge of life into the vastness of death, gasped at the physics of Truth and Beauty. He recognized both as healing agents that can restore our sense of meaning and being in the world. This is all you need in your spiritual first-aid kit. Keep them close to heart and you'll be fine.

This is a fundamental goal of all meaningful education—to impart the wisdom of what Truth and Beauty mean and to explore the skills that can make good use of them. And this is the irrepressible reward for a life of expression—that the truth of our pain and despair will transform itself if we dare to give voice to it. All our endeavors are made more whole for expressing them.

The tragedy of John Keats's short life stands out in literature like a great ballplayer struck down at the beginning of a promising career. We are left wondering what he might have written if he had lived longer. Like wondering how Mickey Mantle would have fared with healthy knees. Or did his courage in facing sudden crisis arc his spirit to the same depths of expression the years would have slowly brought him to?

On February 23, 1821, at the age of 26, John Keats died in Rome. At his wish, he was buried there with an anonymous stone in which these words were carved: *Here lies one whose name was writ in water.* Ironically, the only reason we've found his grave is because his dear friend, the painter Joseph Severn, who cared for him, willed his own burial next to Keats. But on his own stone, Severn had carved, almost pointing to his friend: *Here lies the best friend of John Keats.*

Thankfully, we don't have to die in order to peer into the vastness or to retrieve the wisdom of one whose name was writ in water. We simply need to devote ourselves to being students of Truth and Beauty, letting love stitch them into a rope we can climb or a blanket that can keep us warm.

Truth is necessary to bring us to the edge of transformation, for it forces us to accept the brokenness in our humanness and in the world. From here, we can begin to rearrange and repair.

An Invitation into Your Own Understanding of Beauty and Truth

- In your journal, describe a time when you stumbled into a moment of truth or beauty and what that opened in you. Later, write a poem or story about someone stumbling into a moment of truth or beauty.

- In conversation with a friend or loved one, share an example from your life of something truthful being beautiful and of something beautiful being truthful.

The Wind Phone

On March 11, 2011, a mammoth earthquake triggered a devastating tsunami that wreaked havoc in more than fifteen cities in northeastern Japan. Waves reached as high as 120 feet. More than nineteen thousand people were killed, and twenty-five hundred more have never been found. In thirty minutes, the town of Otsuchi was destroyed.

In trying to make sense of his grief, a gardener from Otsuchi, Itaru Sasaki, said that he needed a place to air his grief. So he moved an empty phone booth into the remnants of his garden and put an old rotary phone on a wooden shelf inside it, even though the phone wasn't connected to anything. Then he dialed his lost loved ones and began to talk to them.

Word spread about the wind phone in Otsuchi, and in time thousands who had lost loved ones in the tsunami made pilgrimage to visit the phone booth in the garden, so they could commune with those they lost through the disconnected phone.

There was the seventy-year-old grandmother who'd lost her husband. She brought her grandchildren so they could tell their grandfather about school. And the fifty-year-old widower who just wept into the phone and listened. And the thirty-three-year-old man who lost his parents, his wife, and his one-year-old son. He dialed the old, battered phone and listened to the wind encircle the booth and finally said, "I don't know what I'm waiting for. . . . I'm so sorry I couldn't save you." And the fifteen-year-old who lost his father, who whispered into the phone, "Why did you have to die?" A month later, he brought his younger sister. She dialed the phone and in her tears, asked, "What happened to your promise to buy me a violin? Now I'll have to buy one myself."

Of course, this story holds great sadness. But when we can listen to the sadness, not skipping over it, until it brings us to the bottom of all feeling, it becomes beautifully clear that it's the power of raw feeling that moves us to express our fundamental being. And the power of that expression is what draws us together to heal. It's the unmitigated depth of expression that releases resilience. This belongs to everyone.

When raw enough, tender enough, and honest enough, we're not ashamed to stand in a phone booth in a garden and speak through the ruins into a phone that isn't connected to anything. From the outside, this may seem like desperation. But having been this desperate, I can attest from the inside—that this reach into the heart of our grief is a courageous act of being that rips through all the excuses we can construct, landing us in the heat and wonder of direct living. And the heart of this courage and the heat and wonder of direct living belong to everyone.

The phone whisperers of Otsuchi are profiles of inner courage. Each of them is a poet. And each of us is a poet, when we dare to swim to the bottom of whatever we feel in order to bring up a taste of what we all have in common. The elixir of our commonness is the reward for diving so deeply and speaking so tenderly.

Thousands who had lost loved ones in the tsunami made pilgrimage to visit the phone booth in the garden, so they could commune with those they lost through the disconnected phone.

An Invitation to Look Back and Listen

- These are the last questions for this journey. In your journal, take each of the twelve section titles in this book and treat each as a doorway to a room. Open the door of each and look into its room and write what you see there. Then, weave the twelve views into one poem, story, or personal reflection.

- In conversation with a friend or loved one, share the twelve views you have recorded, as well as the culminating piece you have written. Then share one thing you will take with you from the long conversation of this book.

This Belongs to Everyone

There's a source deep in the core of human consciousness that's simply a given. It doesn't come from expectations or our beliefs; it's just there, waiting for us to discover—or rediscover—it.
WILLIAM RICHARDS

It's humbling that the path of our expression, in art as in life, always reveals itself after we live it. In looking back, one book after another has led to the next. Exploring awakening led me to the nature of risk, which led me quite naturally to the need to explore courage. After that, there was only to listen. This led me to the endless practice of caring for the soul and for each other. And that led me to try to understand how effort leads to grace. I could never have foreseen such a harmonious unfolding. But this way of learning is not unique to me. This belongs to everyone.

I recently learned of a compelling teaching that comes from the intelligence of nature. After a silkworm encloses itself in its cocoon, it begins to transform, losing the mandibles by which it spun its silky growth chamber. So when the silkworm is ready to emerge as a moth, it has no way to break out of its cocoon. However, during its incandescent gestation, it has developed within its intestine the enzyme serrapeptase, which is so strong that, once regurgitated, it dissolves an opening in the cocoon, through which the moth can emerge into the world.

This is a remarkable metaphor for the life of transformation. From our experience in the world, we build countless forms of cocoons, countless growth chambers in which we gestate until ready to emerge transformed into another, deeper form of self.

But often, what we use to build one chamber of growth will not be able to free us from that chamber of growth. Often, the things in which we grow are only opened by the life of expression. For expression is the powerful enzyme that we must bring up from within in order to dissolve our cocoon, so we can emerge transformed in the same world. This is why we listen and reflect. This is why we write. Not to be accomplished or excellent but to free ourselves from the chambers of our growth, in order to enter the same world transformed. And this holy process belongs to everyone.

Yearning to be, we enter a lifelong process. We follow a thread of connection that reveals itself as a necessary art of being. The unexpected utterance that comes from honest living then helps us lift the veils we encounter. And so, the life of expression helps us keep the world together. This is the purpose of our will, to join the one conversation we all are born to. By seeing one thing in another, we release the Divine Nature in all things and find metaphors to live by. In truth, we relate to things more than we author them.

Though life marks us up, we survive by fitting things together until we inhabit the inner experience of truth. In time, we learn to trust the chord in our heart. Then, it becomes clear that the power of art rests in bearing witness to each other and weaving the threads of life together. Drifting in the immensity, we unravel the riddle of a self. This lets us experience love at first true seeing.

The inescapable truth is that the instrument is you. And keeping the harshness of the world at arm's length, we can dive down and come up, renewed and all ashimmer.

Pulling threads from where we've been and where we feel called to go, we are led not to what is great but what is true. By staying close to what is sacred, we rediscover the covenants of being that surface when we let our life speak. This kind of speech educates the heart.

By giving attention instead of getting attention, we break surface with our soul and find that we are stronger than we thought. And no matter where we find ourselves, effort is never wasted. For this opening of soul that leads to an opening of heart that leads to an opening of voice—all of it is an endless search. And though there is no end to this mystery of being alive, we can find everything we need when going with the stream.

All the while, there is a table between presence and meaning from which we can peer from the edge of all we've lived into what is yet to come. There, we rediscover that what matters comes slowly and, in time, we are brought back to our original sense of wonder, from which we set out again to love the world.

Now we are sitting by the timeless river, as those who have come before us. It is from here that we will know our voice, find our home, and keep going. I will leave you with this.

Wherever I go, I'm blessed to climb with others into the interior we all share. And after a weekend with a group of kind souls, after we've journeyed together honestly, working to listen to each other without judgment but with care—we're closer than when we came together, and what that closeness opens is palpable.

Often, at the end of our time, after I read a last poem, there is a silence that holds us, which is quieter and softer than when we met. Feeling this, I lean into the room and say, "Notice how the silence between us is different now, though we've only been together a short time." Everyone feels it, and no one wants to leave. That's when I lean in further to invite everyone to taste the sweetness in the air. I lean in and say, "Can you feel it? This is what we came for. This is the real poem. This belongs to everyone."

I say this to you now, after our long walk into the River of Light. Lean in a bit further and taste the sweetness we have earned. Can you feel it? This is what we came for. What lives between us is the real poem that enlivens each of us. This drink of luminosity is always within reach. This belongs to everyone.

Gratitudes

My unfailing gratitude to the unseen River of Mystery that, for some strange reason, I have heard my entire life. It keeps coming through me like music through a flute. I would be lost without it. I'm also grateful to my agent Jennifer Rudolph Walsh for her steadfast belief, as well as to Eve Attermann for her endless support, James Munro, Fiona Baird, and the rest of the WME team.

I'm grateful to the Sounds True family, especially Tami Simon for gently inviting me to create the workshop that led to this book, and to my editor, Haven Iverson, and my producer, Steve Lessard, for their care and insight. And to Brooke Warner for our long friendship. And to my publicist Eileen Duhne for her deep commitment. And to Gail Warner, the founder and director of Pine Manor retreat center and my dear friend who, upon reading about the wind phone, had one built.

And to my students. After forty-three years, I feel deeply blessed to have journeyed with so many whose passion of honest inquiry has changed my life, while giving me a companionship of Spirit that I could never have imagined.

And lasting gratitude to my dear friends for the River of Light that is our love. Especially George, Don, Paul, Skip, TC, David, Kurt, Pam, Patti, Karen, Paula, Ellen, Parker, Dave, Jill, Linda, Michelle, Rich, Carolyn, Henk, Sandra, Elesa, Penny, and Joel and Sally. And to Oprah Winfrey for who she is and all she does.

And to Paul Bowler for always being there across the years. And to my dear old friend, Robert Mason, with whom I've peered into Eternity for most of my life. And to my wife, Susan, the words only point to what I feel.

MN

Notes

Epigraphs and poems without attribution are by the author.

The Life of Expression

xv "When power leads towards arrogance, poetry reminds [us] of [our] limitations . . ." This excerpt is from remarks given by John F. Kennedy at Amherst College on October 26, 1963, for the groundbreaking of the Robert Frost Library.

xvi "For authentic, truthful expressions . . ." Notions in this paragraph are from my book of poems, *The Way Under the Way* (Boulder, CO: Sounds True, 2016), xv.

xvi ". . . by way of a journal" For an in-depth guide into the art of journaling, including one hundred journal questions to work with, please see my book *Things That Join the Sea and the Sky: Field Notes on Living* (Boulder, CO: Sounds True, 2017).

Why Write

3 epigraph, "Any 'discovery' we make . . ." From the foreword by W. H. Auden in *Markings* by Dag Hammarskjöld, translated by Leif Sjöberg and W. H. Auden (New York: Vintage Books, 2006), xiii.

The Thread

4 "The Way It Is" From *The Way It Is: New & Selected Poems* by William Stafford (St. Paul, MN: Graywolf Press, 1998), 42.

The Necessary Art

7 "Letters to a Young Poet . . ." Please see *Letters to a Young Poet* by Rainer Maria Rilke, translated by Stephen Mitchell (New York: Modern Library, 2001).

7 "And poetry is . . . intimate with all things" An earlier version of these three paragraphs appeared in "The Necessary Art" in my book of poems *The Way Under the Way*, 2.

9 "For each person is born . . . our way back to God" These four paragraphs appear as "Unlearning Back to God," the January 3 entry in my spiritual daybook *The Book of Awakening*. (San Francisco: Conari Press, 2000).

The Unexpected Utterance

11   "Poetry is not like reasoning . . ." Percy Bysshe Shelley, "A
Defense of Poetry," in *Criticism: The Major Texts*, edited by W. J.
Bate (New York: Harcourt, Brace, Jovanovich, 1970), 433.

A Lifelong Process

15   "Buddhist temples built in the fifth and sixth centuries . . ."
Details here are drawn from the Asian Wing of the Metropolitan
Museum of Art in New York.

Lifting Veils

21   epigraph, "What was any art but a mold . . ." From *The Song of
the Lark* by Willa Cather (New York: CreateSpace Publishing,
2016). Originally published in 1915, part 4, chapter 3.

21   "It is part of a poet's religion . . ." Rabindranath Tagore, from
*The Mahatma and the Poet: Letters and Debates between Gandhi and Tagore
1915–1941*, compiled and edited by Sabyasachi Bhattacharya
(New Delhi, India: National Book Trust, 1997), 166.

22   "a Mayan tale of creation . . ." Retold by Mary-Joan Gerson
in *People of Corn: A Mayan Story* (New York: Little, Brown and
Company, 1995). I am indebted to Margo McLoughlin for
bringing this and so many other ancient tellings into my life.

23   "the power that conceals . . ." M. Hiriyanna in *The Essentials of
Indian Philosophy* (Delhi, India: Motilal Banarsidass, 2000), 25.

23   "describe the Universe . . ." Paul Deussen, *The Philosophy of
the Upanishads*, translated by A. S. Geden (New York: Cosimo
Classics, 2010), 161.

The Gift of Vision

25   epigraph, "The arts are the wilderness areas . . ." Claude
Lévi-Strauss, cited in *The Practice of the Wild* by Gary Snyder
(Berkeley, CA: Counterpoint, 1990), ix.

The Unexpected Dimension

37   "Auguste Rodin started out . . ." Details and quotes from
Rodin's early days are from *You Must Change Your Life: The Story
of Rainer Maria Rilke and Auguste Rodin*, by Rachel Corbett (New
York: Norton, 2016), chapter 3, Kindle version, loc. 485–511.
This is a remarkable book, weaving the evolution of two

creative spirits in ways that uncover the creative impulses that live within each of us.

We Relate More Than We Author

39   epigraph, "I am very interested . . ." Paulus Berensohn was a gentle soul with a clear creative light. As Jonathan Wolfe said in the *New York Times*, "He was a dancer, potter, and teacher whose slower, quieter, more mindful approach to pottery influenced a generation of artists." Berensohn authored the landmark book *Finding One's Way with Clay*. As a dancer, he studied with Merce Cunningham and Martha Graham. As a potter, he was a lifelong friend of the poet-potter M. C. Richards. He taught at Pendle Hill, Swarthmore, and the Penland School of Crafts. Committed to deep ecology, he didn't fire his pots but rather placed them in the forest to melt back into the earth.

39   "I discovered . . ." An earlier version of this paragraph appears in the preface to my book *Finding Inner Courage* (San Francisco: Conari Press, 2007), 6.

41   "The blood of the children . . ." Pablo Neruda, from the poem "I'm Explaining a Few Things" in *Pablo Neruda: Selected Poems, A Bilingual Edition*, translated and edited by Nathaniel Tarn (New York: Dell Publishing, 1972).

42   "Perhaps God . . ." An earlier version of these two paragraphs appear in the chapter "One Living Sense" in my book *Seven Thousand Ways to Listen* (New York: Atria, 2012), 99.

Keeping the World Together

44   "The first story . . ." An earlier version of "The Work of the Worm" appears in my book of stories *As Far As the Heart Can See* (Deerfield Beach, FL: HCI Books, 2012), 57.

46   "The second story . . ." An earlier version of Oscar Wilde's lesson appears in my book *The Endless Practice* (New York: Atria, 2014), 234.

What It Means to Perceive

50   "I dream my painting . . ." Vincent van Gogh, quoted in "Sunbeams" in *The Sun* magazine (issue 428, August 2011), 48.

To See One Thing in Another

56   "Enlightenment is like the moon . . ." From *Moon in a Dewdrop: Writings of Zen Master Dogen*, translated and edited by Kazuaki Tanahashi (San Francisco: North Point Press, 1985), 71.

The Craft of Perception

70   "Artists pursue various methods . . ." Jennifer Blessing, from *Guggenheim Museum: Collection A to Z*, edited by Nancy Spector (New York: Guggenheim Museum Publications, 2009), 164.

73   "How to Write a Poem" Clarissa Pinkola Estés, from *Theatre of the Imagination: Live Performances* (Boulder, CO: Sounds True, 2005), audio CD.

As a Tuning Fork

78   "I am in search of a veena . . ." Rabindranath Tagore, from *The Mahatma and the Poet: Letters and Debates between Gandhi and Tagore 1915–1941*, 80.

79   "Poetry in Japan begins . . ." The quote and the preceding paragraph are from Ki no Tsurayuki's description in Stephen Addiss's *The Art of Haiku: Its History through Poems and Paintings by Japanese Masters*, translated by Stephen Addiss (Boston: Shambhala, 2012), 21–22.

The Inner Experience of Truth

85   "You Ask About Poetry . . ." A poem from my book of poems in progress, *The Song Gives Birth to the Singer*.

86   "I'm in the South Pacific as I write . . ." My friend's letter appeared as part of Oprah's "What I Know For Sure" column in the April 2011 issue of *O, the Oprah Magazine*.

86   "My Life" A poem from my book of poems in progress, *Pictures of the Floating World*.

Feelings Are Paints

91   "Robleto lists his materials . . ." The details are drawn from the showing of Dario Robleto's work as part of a larger exhibit, *Ahistoric Occasion: Artists Making History*, mounted in Fall 2006 at the Massachusetts Museum of Contemporary Art (MASS MoCA) in North Adams.

93   "If I had gone directly . . ." From *Walt Whitman's America: A Cultural Biography* by David S. Reynolds (New York: Vintage Books, 1996), 339.

93   "One looks with the eyes . . ." Rachel Corbett, from *You Must Change Your Life: The Story of Rainer Maria Rilke and Auguste Rodin*, 8.

Fitting Things Together

99   "By trying to create . . ." An earlier version of this paragraph first appeared in "Unraveling the Self" in *Inside the Miracle* (Boulder, CO: Sounds True, 2015), 144.

101   "Up to the age of thirty . . ." From *Charles Darwin: His Life Told in an Autobiographical Chapter and in a Selected Series of his Published Letters*, edited by Francis Darwin (London: William Clowes and Sons, 1892), 51.

Love at First Sight

110   "To be a poet . . . loving is how we get there" An earlier version of this passage first appeared in my book *Seven Thousand Ways to Listen*.

110   "Genius is a crisis . . ." From *Yeats: The Man and The Masks*, by Richard Ellmann (New York: E. P. Dutton & Co., 1958), 186.

Bearing Witness

121   epigraph, "The work of the poet . . ." Diane Ackerman, from the poem "The Work of the Poet Is to Name What Is Holy" in *Origami Bridges* (New York: HarperCollins, 2002).

Looking at Life Together

123   "I regard the Poet . . ." Gandhi, from his essay "The Great Sentinel" in *The Mahatma and the Poet: Letters and Debates between Gandhi and Tagore 1915–1941*, 88.

123   "Mose Allison tells the story . . ." From *Allison Wonderland: The Mose Allison Anthology*, Rhino Records, 1994, liner notes.

The Power of Art

126   epigraph, "Here is a great truth . . ." Helen Luke, *Dark Wood to White Rose* (New York: Parabola Books, 1989), 172–173.

127   "The poet will sing . . ." Gandhi, from his essay "The Great Sentinel" in *The Mahatma and the Poet: Letters and Debates between Gandhi and Tagore 1915–1941*, 23.

128 "referring to Abstract Expressionism . . . as Art of Another Kind" From the exhibit *Art of Another Kind: International Abstraction and the Guggenheim, 1949–1960*, at the Guggenheim Museum, New York, June 2012.

128 "the Automatistes . . ." Inspired by painter Paul-Émile Borduas, and influenced by French poet André Breton's stream-of-consciousness (automatic) style, the Automatistes were devoted to the creative force of the subconscious. The group includes artists such as Jean-Paul Riopelle, Fernand Leduc, Madeleine Arbour, Marcel Barbeau, Bruno Cormier, Claude Gauvreau, Pierre Gauvreau, Muriel Guilbault, Marcelle Ferron, Thérèse Leduc, Jean-Paul Mousseau, Maurice Perron, Louise Renaud, Françoise Riopelle, and dancer Françoise Sullivan.

129 "Abramović . . ." This paragraph is from the chapter "Staying Possible" in my book in progress, *The Temple Is the World*. This chapter explores the brave work of Marina Abramović more deeply.

129 "Balkan Baroque . . ." From the excellent article "Interview: Marina Abramović" by Sean O'Hagan, *The Guardian/The Observer*, October 2, 2010.

130 "based on his experiences . . ." From "Preface to English Edition" by Robert Conquest, in *Prussian Nights: A Narrative Poem* by Alexander Solzhenitsyn, translated by Robert Conquest (London: Collins and Harvill Press, 1977), 6–7.

130 "I needed a clear head . . ." Alexander Solzhenitsyn, quoted in "Books: A Flight into Poetry" by Patricia Blake in *Time*, July 25, 1977.

131 "On July 17, 2005, the *San Francisco Chronicle* . . ." From *Poetry & Commitment: An Essay* by Adrienne Rich (New York: W. W. Norton & Co., 2007), 26–27.

Listening

138 epigraph, "Aloneness is indivisible . . ." Jiddo Krishnamurti, from *Commentaries on Living*, series 1, chapter 5, "Aloneness and Isolation," jkrishnamurti.org/content /series-i-chapter-5-aloneness-and-isolation.

The Instrument That Is You

141   epigraph, "The more faithfully . . ." From *Markings*, Dag Hammarskjöld, translated by Leif Sjöberg and W. H. Auden, 13.

The Quarter Turn

145   epigraph, "I suddenly knew . . ." From *Such Stuff as Dreams Are Made On: The Autobiography and Journals of Helen M. Luke* (New York: Harmony, 2001), 3.

147   "When author Donald Miller asked novelist Toni Morrison . . ." Donald Miller, quoted in "Sunbeams" in *The Sun* magazine (issue 482, February 2016), 48.

The Inner Critic

150   epigraph, "During this period of development . . ." From *Auguste Rodin* by Rainer Maria Rilke, translated by G. Craig Houston (New York: Dover Publications, 2006), 10.

Diving Down and Coming Up

153   "The poet wants to drink from the well of origin . . ." John O'Donohue, from *Beauty: The Invisible Embrace* (New York: Harper Perennial, 2005).

154   "I had a great teacher in all of this . . ." These five paragraphs originally appeared in my book *Finding Inner Courage*, 262. This was my first exploration of the theme "Diving Down and Coming Up."

Love Your Window

157   "Love Your Window" This chapter is a good example of how a theme grabs hold and evolves across years of work. I first encountered "Love Your Window" as a poem in 2012, which appeared in my book *Inside the Miracle*, 202. The poem opened a path to travel down, and I was moved to explore this notion further as a prose chapter in my book *The One Life We're Given* (New York: Atria Books, 2016), 25. I then began discussing the notion of inner windows in my teaching circles, which opened up more terrain. So here I'm entering the conversation one more time.

Breaking Surface

163 epigraph, "Let no one keep you from your journey . . ." From "Breaking Surface" in my book of poems *The Way Under the Way*, 6.

The Endless Search

164 epigraph, "Such is my poetry . . ." Gabriel Celaya, from "Poetry Is a Weapon Loaded with the Future" in *Roots and Wings: Poetry from Spain 1900–1975*, edited and translated by Hardie St. Martin (New York: Harper & Row, 1976), 313.

165 "And along the way . . ." I first explored the notion of the endless search in a chapter by the same name in my book *Seven Thousand Ways to Listen*. And I'm indebted to the pianist and teacher Michael Jones, who first brought the pathways of whole-mind thinking, belonging, and authenticity to my attention when he and I and Judy Brown guided an immersion workshop at the 12th Annual International Leadership Association Conference held in Prague, November 11–14, 2009.

165 "Basho spoke about this to his student, Kikakou . . ." From *A Poet's Journal: Days of 1945–1951* by George A. Seferis, translated by Athan Anagnostopoulos (Cambridge, MA: Harvard University Press, 1974), 59.

Venetian Interior

169 epigraph, "If it doesn't come bursting out . . ." Charles Bukowski, quoted in "Sunbeams" in *The Sun* magazine (issue 472, April 2015), 48.

A Word about Effort

173 "I thought, at first, that real, lasting work . . ." An earlier version of the next four paragraphs originally appeared in the essay "The Phoenix Between Us" in my book of collected essays *Unlearning Back to God: Essays on Inwardness* (London: KNP, 2006), 174–175.

Not Great but True

178 epigraph, "Yesterday I was clever . . ." Rumi, quoted in "Sunbeams" in *The Sun* magazine (issue 495, March 2017), 48.

178   "Giving attention steers us back to center . . ." The first five paragraphs and the last paragraph in this chapter originally appeared in *The Exquisite Risk* (New York: Harmony Books, 2005), 87.

Pulling Threads

187   "I want to speak about a particular way of listening . . ." An earlier version of the next five paragraphs originally appeared in the chapter "Deep Listening" in my book *Seven Thousand Ways to Listen*, 85.

188   "Let me tell you how I try . . ." An earlier version of the next three paragraphs originally appeared in the chapter "Bring Up the Lights" in my book *The One Life We're Given*, 88.

189   "Eudora Welty puts bits and pieces . . ." Ronald A. Sharp, from *The Norton Book of Friendship*, edited by Eudora Welty and Ronald A. Sharp (New York: W. W. Norton, 1991), 27.

190   "There are no mistakes . . ." Stefon Harris, from a TEDSalon talk, New York City, filmed November 2011, posted December 2011 on TED.com.

190   "Incandescence" This poem originally appeared in my book of poems *The Way Under the Way*, 257.

Stacks of Wheat

199   epigraph, "I am certain . . ." From *And There Was Light* by Jacques Lusseyran, translated by Elizabeth R. Cameron (New York: Parabola Books, 1987), 11–12. This is one of the most extraordinary books I have ever read. It is why books are published at all. Also available as an audiobook in Parabola's Audio Library.

200   "Stacks of Wheat" This poem originally appeared in my book of poems *The Way Under the Way*, 146.

202   "Reduced to Joy" This is the title poem from my book *Reduced to Joy* (Berkeley, CA: Viva Editions, 2013), 146.

When the Work Comes Alive

209   epigraph, "There are certain stanzas . . ." Yannis Ritsos, from "Necessary Explanation" in *Yannis Ritsos: Selected Poems 1938–1988*, translated by Kimon Friar and Kostas Myrsiades (Brockport, NY: BOA Editions, 1989), 88. Yannis Ritsos

(1909–1990) is one of the legendary modern Greek poets. Both profound and prolific, Ritsos authored more than 117 books of poetry, translation, fiction, essays, and drama. This seminal collection includes more than twenty-five illustrations of the poet's paintings on rocks.

210 "The Poems . . ." This poem originally appeared in my book of poems *The Way Under the Way*, 251.

The Monkey and the River

214 epigraph, "When people are at a loss . . ." The seventh-century Buddhist monk Hui-neng, from *The Sutra of Hui-neng: Grand Master of Zen*, translated by Thomas Cleary (Boston: Shambhala, 1998), 12.

215 "the mystery of deep listening . . ." I have been working with this quote from Basho for years. I first explored its meaning in the chapter "The Rhythm of Kindness" in my book *The Exquisite Risk*, 169.

The Practice before the Practice

218 "a practice before the practice . . ." An earlier version of the next four paragraphs first appeared in my book *The Endless Practice*, 243.

219 "Poet's Obligation" Stanzas from "Poet's Obligation" in *Selected Poems of Pablo Neruda*, edited by Nathaniel Tarn (New York: Vintage Classics, 2012), 428.

Going with the Stream

222 "Henri Matisse . . ." An earlier version of the stories about Matisse and Monet first appeared in the chapter "The Effort to Keep Looking" in my book *The One Life We're Given*, 236.

Everything We Need

227 "St. Thomas Episcopal Church . . ." In New York City, the church opened on the corner of Broadway and Houston Street in 1826 but burned in 1851. It moved to Fifth Avenue and Fifty-Third Street in 1870, but it also burned in 1905. The current Gothic-style church with its magnificent altar wall opened in 1913. This church, designed by Ralph Adams Cram (1863–1942) and Bertram Grosvenor Goodhue

(1869–1924), was built completely of masonry, without a steel frame.

227 "one of the largest altar screens in the world . . ." The St. Thomas reredos is eighty feet high and forty-three feet wide. When the architect Bertram Goodhue was awarded the American Institute of Architects's gold medal in 1925 for creating *The Great Reredos*, he returned it, requesting that sculptor Lee Lawrie's name be engraved on it with his. Moved by Goodhue's honest welcome, Lawrie said, "Nothing is more precious to an artist than appreciation, nothing harder to share." From *Bertram Grosvenor Goodhue—Architect and Master of Many Arts* by Lee Lawrie et al. (New York: Press of the American Institute, 1925), 34.

228 "There is one notable dead tree . . ." Gerard Manley Hopkins, from his journals, cited in "Hopkins on 'Inscape' and 'Instress'" on The Victorian Web online site by Glenn Everett, last modified 1988: victorianweb.org/authors/hopkins/hopkins1.html.

229 "Listening to a performance of Beethoven's String Quartet no. 14, op. 131 . . ." An earlier version of these four paragraphs originally appeared in the chapter "Without Pause" in my book *The Endless Practice*, 234.

The Magic of Liberty

237 epigraph, "Art brings us into close contact . . ." Henk Brandt, *The Heart of a Pilgrim* (2014), 105 (in manuscript).

Slipping Through

238 "When I was starting out . . ." This passage originally appeared as "The Invitation to Grow" in my book *As Far As the Heart Can See*, 185.

Living in the Gap

243 "Lotte Jacobi" Johanna Alexandra (Lotte) Jacobi (1896–1990) was a German photographer, who immigrated to the United States to escape Nazi Germany. She photographed many luminaries of the twentieth century, including Albert Einstein, Thomas Mann, Robert Frost, Marc Chagall, Eleanor Roosevelt, Alfred Stieglitz, J. D. Salinger, Paul Robeson,

May Sarton, Edward Steichen, W. H. Auden, Martin Buber, W. E. B. Du Bois, Käthe Kollwitz, Peter Lorre, Max Planck, and Chaim Weizmann.

Becoming the Poem

246　"Friedrich Nietzsche . . ." An earlier version of this story originally appeared in the chapter "What Is Necessary?" in my book *Finding Inner Courage*, 267.

The Empty Saddle

250　"The artist has a right . . ." From *Auguste Rodin* by Rainer Maria Rilke, translated by G. Craig Houston, 16.

250　"His work alone spoke to him . . ." From *Auguste Rodin* by Rainer Maria Rilke, translated by G. Craig Houston, 10.

252　"One of my favorite images comes from Basho . . ." I first told this story in the chapter "The Gift and the Saddle" in my book *The Exquisite Risk*, 276.

What Matters Comes Slowly

256　epigraph, "It does not do to hurry" Rodin, from *Auguste Rodin*, by Rainer Maria Rilke, translated by G. Craig Houston, 5.

256　"It is difficult to get the news . . ." William Carlos Williams, from "Asphodel, That Greeny Flower" in *Asphodel, That Greeny Flower and Other Love Poems* (New York: New Directions, 1994).

256　"God make me . . ." From *E. E. Cummings: Complete Poems 1904–1962*, edited by George James Firmage (New York: Liveright, 1991), 1069.

257　"To Paint the Portrait of a Bird" By Jacques Prévert, from *Modern European Poetry*, edited by Willis Barnstone, translated by John Dixon Hunt (New York: Bantam Books, 1978), 49.

259　"How many thousands of poems . . ." By Su Tung-P'o, from *Selected Poems of Su Tung-P'o*, translated by Burton Watson (Port Townsend, WA: Copper Canyon Press, 1993). Su Tung-P'o was a writer, poet, artist, calligrapher, pharmacologist, and statesman of the Song Dynasty, and one of the major poets of the Song era. Close to 2,700 of Su Tung-P'o's poems have survived, along with 800 of his letters.

The Table Between Presence and Meaning

261   epigraph, "If I could tell you what it meant . . ." Isadora Duncan, from *The Traveler's Journal*, edited by Lim and Sam Shapiro (Bali: Half Angel Press, 2007), 45.

The Wind Phone

270   "In trying to make sense of his grief . . ." Details about the wind telephone of Otsuchi are from the podcast *This American Life* hosted by Ira Glass, episode 597, act 1, "One Last Thing Before I Go," produced by Miki Meek, September 23, 2016. The original report was filmed by a Japanese TV crew from NHK Sendai.

This Belongs to Everyone

273   epigraph, "There's a source . . ." William Richards is quoted in "From Here to Eternity: William Richards on the Transformative Potential of Psychedelics" by Mark Leviton, in *The Sun* magazine (issue 503, November 2017), 8.

273   "After a silkworm encloses itself in its cocoon . . ." I learned about the enzyme serrapeptase and its origin from my dear friend Henk Brandt, a Renaissance man whose heart and mind are vast and deep.

275   "let our life speak" For a profound and tender example of the power of personal expression opening a well of common wisdom, please read Parker J. Palmer's modern classic, *Let Your Life Speak: Listening for the Voice of Vocation* (San Francisco: Jossey-Bass, 1999).

Permissions

About the Author

Mark Nepo moved and inspired readers and seekers all over the world with his #1 *New York Times* bestseller, *The Book of Awakening*. Beloved as a poet, teacher, and storyteller, Mark has been called "one of the finest spiritual guides of our time," "a consummate storyteller," and "an eloquent spiritual teacher." His work is widely accessible and used by many; his books have been translated into more than twenty languages. A bestselling author, he has published twenty-one books and recorded fourteen audio projects. In 2015, he was given a Life-Achievement Award by AgeNation. In 2016, he was named by *Watkins Mind Body Spirit* as one of the 100 Most Spiritually Influential Living People, and he was also chosen as one of OWN's SuperSoul 100, a group of inspired leaders using their gifts and voices to elevate humanity. And in 2017 Mark became a regular columnist for *Spirituality & Health Magazine*.

Recent work includes *More Together Than Alone: Discovering the Power and Spirit of Community in Your Life and in the World* (Atria, 2018), cited by *Spirituality & Practice* as one of the Best Spiritual Books of 2018; *Things That Join the Sea and the Sky* (Sounds True, 2017), a Nautilus Book Award Winner; *The Way Under the Way: The Place of True Meeting* (Sounds True, 2016), a Nautilus Book Award Winner; *The One Life We're Given* (Atria, 2016), cited by Spirituality & Practice as one of the Best Spiritual Books of 2016; *Inside the Miracle* (Sounds True, 2015), selected by *Spirituality & Health Magazine* as one of the Top Ten Best Books of 2015; *The Endless Practice* (Atria, 2014), cited by Spirituality & Practice as one of the Best Spiritual Books of 2014; and *Seven Thousand Ways to Listen* (Atria, 2012), which won the 2012 Books for a Better Life Award.

Mark was part of Oprah Winfrey's The Life You Want tour in 2014 and has appeared several times with Oprah on her *Super Soul Sunday* program on OWN TV. He has also been interviewed by Robin Roberts on *Good Morning America*. Spirituality & Practice cited *The Exquisite Risk* as one of the Best Spiritual Books of 2005, calling it "one of the best books we've ever read on what it takes to live an authentic life."

Mark devotes his writing and teaching to the journey of inner transformation and the life of relationship. He continues to offer readings, lectures, and retreats. Please visit Mark at marknepo.com, threeintentions.com, and wmespeakers.com/speaker/mark-nepo.

About Sounds True

Sounds True is a multimedia publisher whose mission is to inspire and support personal transformation and spiritual awakening. Founded in 1985 and located in Boulder, Colorado, we work with many of the leading spiritual teachers, thinkers, healers, and visionary artists of our time. We strive with every title to preserve the essential "living wisdom" of the author or artist. It is our goal to create products that not only provide information to a reader or listener, but that also embody the quality of a wisdom transmission.

For those seeking genuine transformation, Sounds True is your trusted partner. At SoundsTrue.com you will find a wealth of free resources to support your journey, including exclusive weekly audio interviews, free downloads, interactive learning tools, and other special savings on all our titles.

To learn more, please visit SoundsTrue.com/freegifts or call us toll-free at 800.333.9185.

sounds true
WAKING UP THE WORLD